Designing React Hooks the Right Way

Explore design techniques and solutions to debunk
the myths about adopting states using React Hooks

Fang Jin

BIRMINGHAM—MUMBAI

Designing React Hooks the Right Way

Associate Group Product Manager: Pavan Ramchandani

Publishing Product Manager: Aaron Tanna

Senior Editor: Sofi Rogers

Content Development Editor: Rakhi Patel

Technical Editor: Joseph Aloocaran

Copy Editor: Safis Editing

Project Coordinator: Manthan Patel

Proofreader: Safis Editing

Indexer: Subalakshmi Govindhan

Production Designer: Alishon Mendonca

Marketing Coordinator: Teny Thomas

First published: December 2021

Production reference: 1101221

Published by Packt Publishing Ltd.

Livery Place

35 Livery Street

Birmingham

B3 2PB, UK.

ISBN 978-1-80323-595-0

www.packt.com

To my wife, Maggie, for her love, care, and support for the whole family, and to my two wonderful kids, Sophia and Lucas, for their curiosity and inspiration. To my parents, Qiang and Yunxia, for the sacrifices they made for me. To everyone else who has supported me.

To my grandpa, Jingzhen Jin, as my life's mentor and role model.

– Fang Jin

Foreword

I have known Fang professionally and personally. He has a genuine personality and is an excellent technologist. We have built multiple applications together for one of the major financial firms where he was UI/UX Lead and Architect. His designed & developed generic framework has been used by many applications in our organization. His fondness and expertise in UI/UX were evident to everyone, and he is always enthusiastic in developing new components and cognizant about newer technologies in UI space. Personally, I have not only learnt from him about using the available technology as-is but also understanding it in depth to grow your knowledge. His years of freelancing work and contribution in UI open-source community is incredible and we always anticipated that he will be a big help in this global UI community, which is coming out now by his book. The book will surely benefit many people.

Sagar Kale

Technology Manager, Deutsche Bank

Contributors

About the author

Fang Jin is a software engineer who makes reusable and scalable web modules that can be applied to modern browsers and devices. He is an engineering hobbyist with interests ranging from economics and philosophy to software development, architecture, and team development. Fang is a lifelong learner and throughout his journey, he has helped organizations and teams adopt UI frameworks to achieve consistent branding and look and feel across departments so that they can save costs and boost efficiency. In his free time, he likes swimming and surfing YouTube.

While the task of writing a book may seem like a personal adventure, this book simply could not have happened without the editorial team.

I especially want to thank my Editors, Sofi Rogers and Rakhi Patel; you've shown me how a book should be written, and your insights have sharpened each chapter. I also want to thank my Product Managers, Pavan Ramchandani and Aaron Tanna, who actually made the book possible. Since the past 8 years, I have been a loyal reader of the books published by Packt and it makes me happy that I could contribute to Packt Publishing from my end.

About the reviewers

Mikhail Sakhniuk is a software engineer with high proficiency in JavaScript, React, and React Native. He has more than 5 years of experience in developing web and mobile applications. He has experience with start-ups, fintech, and product companies that have more than 20 million users. Currently, Mikhail is working at Miro as a frontend engineer. Also, he owns and maintains a few open source projects. His experience and skills are shared via articles and books.

Michael Asiedu is a full stack JavaScript developer who is hellbent on creating radical outcomes and web apps that scale. His passion for coding, books, and writing has fueled the release of great technical articles and ebooks in the tech community. Before entering software development, he worked in digital marketing, where he co-founded a digital marketing agency with three of his high school friends. Michael has a solid JavaScript background and he sees himself venturing into the Web 3.0 industry. He is a big advocate of open source.

Table of Contents

3
Hooking into React

4
Use State to Jumpstart Components

5
Use Effect to Handle Side Effects

6

Use Memo to Boost Performance

7

Use Context to Cover an Area

8
Use Ref to Hide Stuff

9
Use Custom Hooks to Reuse Logic

10

Building a Website with React

Preface

React has been my main development tool lately. In my experience both as a developer and a computer user, I found most of what I love in the end is non-heavy stuff. While big names come and go often, there're certain things left behind. For instance, the way to build a website has been reshaped and refined over the past twenty years, but the general process of building it hasn't changed much. You still need to create an *HTML* file, design the layout, and host it somewhere on a server.

When it comes to the **user interface** (**UI**), there's another topic that can benefit you in a similar way. That is state. From *jQuery* and *Angular* to *React*, from the web to other non-desktop platforms (such as *Electron* or *React Native*), no matter where you go, there's a technical question that you need to answer now – *how does the screen know there's a change to apply?* When I was back in college, I never asked this type of question. I generally assumed the computer just worked that way.

Of course, now I know the computer works that way because someone made it. What's fascinating about the UI is when the state gets in the picture. Back in the early days, we didn't talk about state at all. But now state is everywhere, although there's still no textbook definition for it or how we should learn it in the first place. Suffice to say, state is still a relatively young topic in the web development industry.

In this book, I'll attempt, by using *React* as the underlying technology, to explore and learn how states are introduced and implemented. I hope, by doing that, we will have a better picture in the end to answer the question – *how is a render engine driven by states?*

Who this book is for

The ideal reader of this book is an engineer who has been writing *JavaScript* for a few years but doesn't necessarily have experience with *React* and/or the function component. For readers with less *JavaScript* experience, we include a live playground via *CodePen* so that you can experiment with each topic in no time.

If you do have experience with *React*, or even Hooks, that's fine; this book will show you how Hooks are implemented within the function component. Moreover, a stripped-down version of the *React* source code pertaining to each Hook is also included in each chapter, so you will get a deeper understanding if you are an experienced *React* programmer.

What this book covers

Chapter 1, Introducing the Function Component, explains what a function component is with an explanation of its props and the basic parent/child relationship. You will then get some tips on how to write a function component. At the end of the chapter, you will see a practical function component example, Nav.

Chapter 2, Crafting States in Functions, shows how to craft a special variable called state in function components. We will see what benefits a state can provide, including requesting a new update and listening to a value change. We will also see an example of applying a state to a **Single Page Application (SPA)**. We will also take a close look at what role states play in the *UI*.

Chapter 3, Hooking into React, goes through the challenges we face when creating a good state solution, and then we'll see how *React* architects provide the solution with the underlying Hook. We will then introduce Hooks, learn about their calling order, and learn how to avoid running into the conditional Hook issue in real applications.

Chapter 4, Use State to Jumpstart Components, covers built-in Hooks, starting with the useState Hook. We will first explain how state is used in *React* and then walk through the data structure and source code behind useState, and we'll also describe common usages of dispatching states. We'll give useState a test drive and provide two practical examples of applying useState to the Avatar and Tooltip components.

Chapter 5, Use Effect to Handle Side Effects, introduces side effects, walks through the data structure and source code behind useEffect, and provides various scenarios in which you invoke effects. We will also demonstrate a couple of pitfalls of using useEffect and ways to avoid them. And we'll use useEffect in two practical examples, Window Size and a Fetch API.

Chapter 6, Use Memo to Boost Performance, explains how we can run into performance degradation issues in a typical web application. Then we will walk through the design and source code behind useMemo and describe various ways of reusing a value conditionally. We'll then apply the optimization technique to two common cases, clicking to search and debouncing the search.

Chapter 7, Use Context to Cover an Area, introduces an area updates and how *React* contexts are used to share a value to an area. Then, we will walk through the data structure and source code behind `useContext` to consume the shared value. At the end of the chapter, we'll provide two practical examples of applying contexts to a Theme and a Table.

Chapter 8, Use Ref to Hide Stuff, explains how to access a *DOM* element via a ref, and we'll walk through the design and source code behind the `useRef` Hook. We will also describe how to work with a persistent value without dispatching an update. Finally, we'll apply refs to a couple of practical problems, such as clicking outside of the menu, avoiding memory leaks, setting up a mule, and locating the current value.

Chapter 9, Use Custom Hooks to Reuse Logic, gathers all the Hooks we have learned about so far and explains how to create a custom Hook for our own needs. We will introduce custom Hooks and then write a couple of custom Hooks step by step, including `useToggle`, `useWindow`, `useAsync`, `useDebounced`, `useClickOutside`, `useCurrent`, and `useProxy`.

Chapter 10, Building a Website with React, discusses *React* in general, especially the role *React* plays in web development. We will approach this topic from three perspectives to see how *React* puts resources together to build a site, including *JavaScript ES6* features, *CSS-in-JS* approaches, and the transformation from *HTML*-like lines into *JavaScript* expressions.

To get the most out of this book

One of the goals of this book is for you to get hands-on experience using *React* and Hooks. Following are a couple of options that you can follow to get the most out of the content before you start.

Refresh your knowledge of React

If you haven't used *React* lately or are not familiar with its cutting-edge features, I recommended you jump to *Chapter 10, Building a Website with React*, to get an overview of the three building blocks that *React* relies upon to build a website: JavaScript, CSS, and HTML.

While reading the book, feel free to visit this chapter often if you run into new syntax that you are not familiar with, or you simply want to gain more insights into how each building block is utilized in *React*.

Use a browser without building the code

If you don't have a local environment to work with the code or you simply don't want to build the code, you can access the examples from an online server at `https://codepen.io/windmaomao/pen/ExvYPEX`. You should get `Hello World` printed on your screen in no time. Each chapter comes with a couple of playground links that you can click to follow. They appear as follows in the book:

Playground – Hello World

Feel free to play with this online example at `https://codepen.io/windmaomao/pen/ExvYPEX`.

Build the code yourself

If you are a hands-on person and would like to follow the code step by step in each chapter, you need to have *React* installed in one of your projects. Instructions to set up a *React* project from scratch are as follows.

npm

Visit the Node.js website, `https://nodejs.org`, to grab the latest versions of `Node.js` and `npm`. Pick the right version for your operating system and install it. To find out if everything has been installed properly, open a terminal, and run the following command:

```
node -v
```

If you see a version number returned by the preceding command, Node.js has been installed.

Create React App

You can get your *React* project up and running quickly by using the following command:

```
npx create-react-app my-app
```

Replace `my-app` with your desired application name. Once you have the projects ready, you can go into the `my-app` folder and launch it:

```
cd my-app
yarn start
```

That's it, you should see an application on your local computer. Now you can try the source code out by pasting our code over your project and compiling it locally.

Download the color images

We also provide a PDF file that has color images of the screenshots and diagrams used in this book. You can download it here: `https://static.packt-cdn.com/downloads/9781803235950_ColorImages.pdf`.

Conventions used

There are a number of text conventions used throughout this book.

`Code in text`: Indicates code words in text, database table names, folder names, filenames, file extensions, pathnames, dummy URLs, user input, and Twitter handles. Here is an example: "The element can be as simple as `h1`, a `div` element, or it can be an artificial element that does things differently."

A block of code is set as follows:

```
fetch('/giveMeANumber').then(res => {
  ReactDOM.render(<Title />, rootEl)
})
```

When we wish to draw your attention to a particular part of a code block, the relevant lines or items are set in bold:

```
let c = 3

function add(a, b) {
  console.log(a, b)
  return a + b + c
}
```

Bold: Indicates a new term, an important word, or words that you see onscreen. For instance, words in menus or dialog boxes appear in **bold**. Here is an example: "This flag can be used to decide if the UI should display the **Logout** or **Login** button."

> **Tips or Important Notes**
> Appear like this.

Get in touch

Feedback from our readers is always welcome.

General feedback: If you have questions about any aspect of this book, email us at customercare@packtpub.com and mention the book title in the subject of your message.

Errata: Although we have taken every care to ensure the accuracy of our content, mistakes do happen. If you have found a mistake in this book, we would be grateful if you would report this to us. Please visit www.packtpub.com/support/errata and fill in the form.

Piracy: If you come across any illegal copies of our works in any form on the internet, we would be grateful if you would provide us with the location address or website name. Please contact us at copyright@packt.com with a link to the material.

If you are interested in becoming an author: If there is a topic that you have expertise in and you are interested in either writing or contributing to a book, please visit authors.packtpub.com.

Share Your Thoughts

Once you've read *Designing React Hook the Right Way*, we'd love to hear your thoughts! Scan the QR code below to go straight to the Amazon review page for this book and share your feedback.

https://packt.link/r/1803235950/

Your review is important to us and the tech community and will help us make sure we're delivering excellent quality content.

1
Introducing the Function Component

In this chapter, we will first start with a brief history of *UI* components developed over the past two decades and get to know how *React* uses *UI* components to put together an application. You will learn what a function component is, with an explanation of its props and the basic parent/child relationship. You will then get some tips on how to write a function component. At the end, you will see a practical function component example, `Nav`. The chapter also includes one bonus topic in the *Appendix* section: *How many component types does React support?*

We will cover the following topics in this chapter:

- History of *UI* components
- Building an app with components
- Introducing the function component
- Writing a function component
- Example of a function component

- Questions and answers
- Appendix

History of UI components

While we are fascinated by technology, it can also be intriguing to watch how slowly it evolves over time. In our case, it's *HTML*. On the surface, it doesn't appear to have changed for the past 20 years. You get that idea by comparing a typical web page written now with one written 20 years ago, and seeing that they look very similar, if not identical.

The following snippet shows what typical *HTML* page code looks like:

```
<HTML>
  <head>
    <meta charset="utf-8">
  </head>
  <style>
    h1 { color: red; }
  </style>
  <script>
    console.log('start...')
  </script>
  <body>
    <h1>Hello World</h1>
  </body>
</HTML>
```

Those of us who have been in this industry long enough know that the web has been reshaped a couple of times. In particular, a tremendous amount of effort has been spent on how to generate the preceding *HTML*.

Web engineers have tried to divide the file up into multiple parts, including *HTML*, *JavaScript*, and *CSS*, and then put it back together upon rendering the file onscreen. They have also tried to load one or two parts on servers, and the rest on client computers. They have also tried various compilers or builders to autogenerate the file after each change to the source code. They have tried lots of things. Actually, almost anything you can think of regarding *HTML* has been tried a couple of times in the past, and people will not stop trying something just because someone else has tried it. In a sense, web technology gets re-invented every once in a while.

With so much new content being added to the web every day, engineers have found the *HTML* files a bit unmanageable. On the one hand, the demand is that users want to see more actionable items with quicker responses and, on the other hand, many of these actionable items on the screen create challenges for engineers to manage the workload and maintain the code base.

So, engineers are on a constant lookout for better ways to organize *HTML* files. If this organization is done right, it can help them not get overwhelmed by a plethora of elements on the screen. At the same time, organizing files well means a scalable project, since the team can divide the project into smaller pieces and work on each in a divide-and-conquer way.

Let's take a look at the history of how technologies using *JavaScript* assisted with these topics. We will choose four technologies for this conversation – *jQuery*, *Angular*, *React*, and *LitElement*.

jQuery

jQuery is a library used to manipulate the **Document Object Model** (**DOM**) elements on the screen. It recognizes the challenges of working with the *DOM* directly, thereby providing a utility layer to simplify the syntax of finding, selecting, and manipulating *DOM* elements. It was developed in 2006 and has been used by millions of websites since then.

What's great about jQuery is that it can work with an existing *HTML* by creating a wrapper around it using the famous $ symbol, as you can see in the following code:

```
$(document).ready(function(){
  $("button").click(function(){
    $(this).css("background-color", "yellow");
    $("#div3").fadeIn(3000);
    $("#p1").css("color", "red")
      .slideUp(2000)
      .slideDown(2000);
  });
});

function appendText() {
  var txt1 = "<p>Text.</p>";
  var txt2 = $("<p></p>").text("Text.");
  var txt3 = document.createElement("p");
  txt3.innerHTML = "Text.";
  $("body").append(txt1, txt2, txt3);
}
```

jQuery didn't have much competition when it came to changing color, font, or any attribute of an element at runtime. It made it possible to organize large chunks of business logic code into functions stored in multiple files. It also provided a modular way to create reusable UI widgets through one of its plugins at the time.

Complete separation between *HTML* and *JavaScript* was strongly favored back then. At that time, people believed that this way of doing things helped to raise productivity, since people who work with website styles and behaviors can be from two departments. Theming, the word describing the application of style to a site, was gaining popularity and some jobs were looking for developers who could make a site look as beautiful as a Photoshop design.

Angular

Angular is a web framework used to develop a **Single-Page Application (SPA)**. It was invented by *Google* in 2010. It was quite revolutionary at the time, because you could build a frontend application with it. This means that the code written in *Angular* could take over the body of *HTML* and apply logic to all elements within it at runtime. All code was run at the browser level, resulting in the word "frontend" starting to appear in job résumés. Since then, web developers have been roughly categorized as "backend," "frontend," and "full stack" (which means both frontend and backend).

The code that *Angular* uses continues to be built on existing *HTML* by attaching additional tags to it like so:

```
<body>
  <div ng-app="myApp" ng-controller="myCtrl">
    <p>Name: <input type="text" ng-model="name" /></p>
  </div>
  <script>
    var app = angular.module('myApp', []);
    app.controller('myCtrl', function($scope) {
      $scope.name= "John";
    });
  </script>
</body>
```

The controller and module introduced by *Angular* can imbue business logic to sections of *HTML* with unique scopes. *Angular* supports components and directives out of the box, which allows us to reference all relevant *HTML* and *JavaScript* together in a single file (although the *HTML* file still needs to be written in a separate file):

```
function HeroListController($scope, $element, $attrs) {
  var ctrl = this;
```

```
  ctrl.updateHero = function(hero, prop, value) {
    hero[prop] = value;
  };

  ctrl.deleteHero = function(hero) {
    var idx = ctrl.list.indexOf(hero);
    if (idx >= 0) {
      ctrl.list.splice(idx, 1);
    }
  };
}

angular.module('heroApp').component('heroList', {
  templateUrl: 'heroList.html',
  controller: HeroListController
});
```

The component created via Angular can be reused afterward in an HTML file.

React

React, also known as *React.js*, was developed by *Facebook* and released in 2013 as a *JavaScript* library for building *UI* components. Although it wasn't specifically marketed as a web framework, it has been used by developers to build single-page or mobile applications, and has been favored by start-up companies in particular ever since.

What was controversial at the time was how it treated *HTML* statements. Instead of leaving them in a *HTML* file, it actually asked to take them out and put under a `render` function of a component, like so:

```
<div id="root"></div>

<script type="text/babel">
  class App extends React.Component {
    render() {
      return <h1>Hello World</h1>
    }
  }
  ReactDOM.render(App, document.getElementById('root'));
</script>
```

This unique approach favors the component design much more than the integrity of the *HTML* file. This was (almost) the first time you could put *HTML* and *JavaScript* together under the same file. We call it *HTML* here because it looks like *HTML*, but actually *React* creates a wrapper to transform the *HTML* into *JavaScript* statements.

When *React* was introduced, it came with a class component and in 2015, it added support for a function component, so you can write the logic under a function instead of a class:

```
<script type="text/babel">
  const App = function() {
    return <h1>Hello World</h1>
  }
</script>
```

With *React*, the *HTML* files don't get touched as often as they used to be; in fact, they don't get changed at all, since the *HTML* content is all relocated to *React* components. This approach can still be controversial today because people who don't care about the location of the *HTML* would get onboard very easily, whereas people who care about the classical way of writing *HTML* would stay away. There's also a mentality shift here; with *React*, *JavaScript* becomes the focus of web development.

LitElement

Polymer was developed by *Google* and released in 2015, designed to build web applications using web components. In 2018, the *Polymer* team announced that any future development would be shifted to *LitElement* to create fast and lightweight web components:

```
@customElement('my-element')
export class MyElement extends LitElement {
  ...
  render() {
    return html`
      <h1>Hello, ${this.name}!</h1>
      <button @click=${this._onClick}>
        Click Count: ${this.count}
      </button>
      <slot></slot>
    `;
  }
}
```

There are quite a few similarities between *React* and *LitElement* since it allows you to define a class component with a `render` function. What's unique about *LitElement* is that once the element is registered, it can behave like a DOM element:

```html
<body>
  <h1>Hello World</h1>
  <my-element name="abc">
    <p>
      Let's get started.
    </p>
  </my-element>
</body>
```

There's no apparent entry point for integrating *LitElement* into *HTML* since it doesn't need to gain control of a `body` element before using it. We can design the element somewhere else, and when it comes to its use, it's more like using an `h1` element. Therefore, it perfectly preserves the integrity of the HTML file while outsourcing the additional capability to the custom element, which can be designed by others.

The goal of *LitElement* is to have the web component work in any web page within any framework.

20 years ago, we didn't know what the web would become. From this brief historical review of *jQuery*, *Angular*, *React*, and *LitElement*, it's clear that an idea of having *UI* components has emerged. A component, like a block of LEGO, can do the following:

- Encapsulate functionalities inside

- Be reused in other places

- Not jeopardize the existing site

Thus, when we use the component, it takes the following syntax:

```html
<component attr="Title">Hello World</component>
```

Essentially, this isn't too different from where we started with writing *HTML*:

```html
<h1 title="Title">Hello World</h1>
```

There's a hidden requirement for a component here. While the components can be designed separately, in the end, they have to be put together to serve a higher purpose, to finish building a site. Therefore, as atomic as each component is, there still needs to be a communication layer to allow blocks to talk to one another.

As long as components are functioning and there is communication between them, the app can function as a whole. This is actually the assumption of a component design along with building a site.

So, into what category does our book fall? Our book is about building components under *React*, especially building smart components that can serve as a reusable block and are able to fit in an app. The technology we have chosen here is hooks inside a function component.

Before we get into the details of components and hooks, let's first take a brief look at how components can be put together to build an application.

Building an app with components

To start building an application, here's a block of *HTML* you can start with:

```
<!doctype HTML>
<HTML lang="en">
  <body>
    <div id="root"></div>
  </body>
</HTML>
```

These days, we have more and more **SPAs** that update parts of pages on the fly, which makes using the website feel like a native application. A quick response time is what we are aiming for. JavaScript is the language to deliver this goal, from displaying the user interface to running application logic and communicating with the web server.

To add logic, React takes over one section of the HTML to start a component:

```
<script>
  const App = () => {
    return <h1>Hello World.</h1>
  }
  const rootEl = document.getElementById("root")
  ReactDOM.render(<App />, rootEl)
</script>
```

The render function in the preceding code, provided by ReactDOM, accepts two input arguments, which are a *React* element and a *DOM* element, rootEl. rootEl is where you want *React* to render, in our case, a *DOM* node tagged with the root ID. What *React* renders to rootEl can be found defined in a function component, App.

It's important to tell the difference between App and <App /> in *React*. App is a component, and there has to be a definition out there to describe what it can do:

```
const App = () => {
  return <h1>Hello World</h1>
}
```

Whereas <App /> is one instance of the App component. A component can have lots of instances created from it, quite similar to the instance of a class in most programming languages. Creating an instance out of a component is the first step to reusability.

If we launch the preceding code in a browser, we should see it display the following **Hello World** title:

Hello World

Figure 1.1 – Hello World

> **Playground – Hello World**
>
> Feel free to play with this example online at `https://codepen.io/windmaomao/pen/ExvYPEX`.

To have a fully functional application, normally we would need more than one page. Let's take a look at a second page.

Multiple pages

Building a "Hello World" component is the first step. But how does a single component like that support multiple pages so that we can navigate from one page to another?

Say we have two pages, both defined in components, Home and Product:

```
const Home = () => {
  return <h1>Home Page</h1>
}

const Product = () => {
  return <h1>Product Page</h1>
}
```

To display either `Home` or `Product`, we can create a helper component:

```
const Route = ({ home }) => {
  return home ? <Home /> : <Product />
}
```

The preceding `Route` component is a bit different; it carries an input argument, `home`, from the function definition. `home` holds a Boolean value and based on it, the `Route` component can switch between displaying `<Home />` or `<Product />`.

Now it's a matter of determining what the value for `home` in `App` is:

```
const App = () => {
  const home = true
  return <Route home={home} />
}
```

In the preceding code, the `App` component is amended to include a `home` variable, which gets passed to the `Route` component.

You might have noticed that the current code will only display the Home page because we have set `home` to `true`. Don't worry. This whole book is about teaching you how to set the `home` value. For now, just imagine the value would be flipped from `true` to `false` based on a user mouse click, and for the time being, you can manually change the `home` value.

The `App` component can grow bigger as more and more components are added underneath it with this routing mechanism. This is partly why the first component in a *React* application is named `App`. Although you can name it whatever you want, just remember to use a capitalized letter for the first letter.

Playground – Home Page

Feel free to play with the example online at `https://codepen.io/` `windmaomao/pen/porzgOy`.

Now we can see how *React* puts together an app, so without further ado, let's get to the component in *React*.

There are mainly two component types that *React* supports – a class component and a function component. This book will focus on a function component. If you are interested in other component types, please check out the *Appendix A – How many component types does React support?* section at the end of this chapter.

Introducing the function component

"This pattern is designed to encourage the creation of these simple components that should comprise large portions of your apps."
– Sophie Alpert

In this section, we are going to introduce you to the function component. When the function component was first introduced in React 0.14 in August 2015, it was named as a stateless pure function:

```
function StatelessComponent(props) {
  return <div>{props.name}</div>
}
```

The main intention was that "stateless pure-function components give us more opportunity to make performance optimizations."

A function component with no state, by default, is designed to take the following function form:

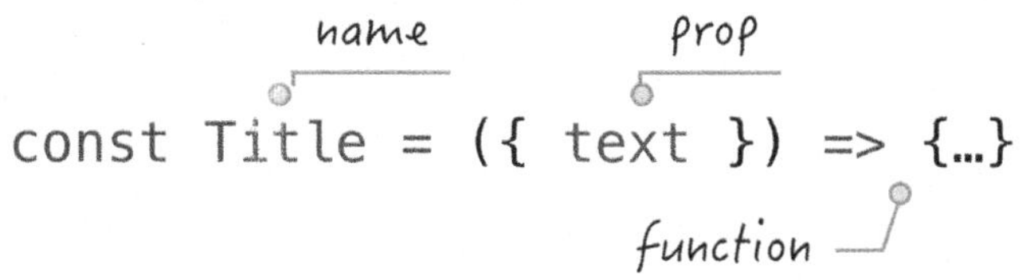

Figure 1.2 – Function component definition

We are going to explore parts of a function component in detail in the next subsections.

Function props

The input argument of this function is referred to as a prop. Props take an object format under which we can define any property. Each property is referred to as a prop. For instance, *Figure 1.2* defines a `Title` component with a `text` prop.

Because props are objects, there's no limitation to how many props can be defined under that object:

```
const Title = ({ name, onChange, on, url }) => {...}
```

The job of a prop, similar to an input argument, is to pass a value to the function. There is also no limitation in terms of the type of prop. Since each prop is a property of an object, it can be a string, a number, an object, a function, an array, or anything that can be assigned using a *JavaScript* expression, as in the following example:

```
const Title = ({ obj }) => {
  return <h1>{obj.text}</h1>
}

const Title = ({ fn }) => {
  return <h1>{fn()}</h1>
}
```

In the preceding code, the first case passes an `obj` prop carrying a `text` property, while the second case passes an `fn` prop that gets invoked inside.

Once a function component has been defined, it can be used as many times as you want in other places via its instances:

```
const App = () => {
  return <Title text="Hello World" />
}
```

In the preceding code, a `Title` component instance is used in the definition of an `App` component.

And when the `App` component is updated, a string, `"Hello World"`, is assigned to the `text` prop of the `Title` component. The usage of the `Title` component reminds us of the *HTML* statement, and the `text` prop reminds us of the attribute of the *DOM* element.

We have actually seen the usage of an `App` component instance as well at the beginning:

```
    ReactDOM.render(<App />, rootEl)
```

In short, you can define a component, but to see what it displays on the screen, its instance needs to be used.

Children prop

All the props of a function component should be defined explicitly, just like input arguments. But, there's a prop worth knowing early on that isn't apparent to follow this rule. This is called a `children` prop:

```
const App = () => {
  return (
    <Title>
```

```
      Hello World
    </Title>
  )
}
```

You might be using the preceding code without knowing how exactly the `"Hello World"` string is put under the `Title` component. Interestingly, the string is wired to the component via a `children` prop. This will become clear when we get to the definition of the `Title` component:

```
const Title = ({ children }) => {
  return <h1>{children}</h1>
}
```

Essentially, the `App` component takes `"Hello World"` and assigns it to the `children` prop before invoking the `Title` component instance. You might wonder what happens if we forget to include the `children` prop when defining the `Title` component:

```
const Title = () => {
  return <h1>Haha, you got me</h1>
}
```

In that case, `"Hello World"` is ignored and the `App` component reduces to the following case:

```
const App = () => {
  return <Title />
}
```

Apparently, this is not intended since, if you put children elements under a component, then a `children` prop has to be defined explicitly in the function definition. This means that a `children` prop still needs to be explicitly written on the function interface.

In fact, the `children` prop is the reason why a component can be nested under another component. *React* uses this `children` mechanism to reproduce how the *HTML* writes in general.

Parent and child

In *React*, props are the mechanism for components talking to one another. We can generalize this idea by using two components normally involved in the communication to a parent and a child, as we have already seen in `App` and `Title`:

```
const Title = ({ text }) => {
  return <h1>{text}</h1>
}
```

```
  }

const App = ({ flag }) => {
  const text = flag ? "Hello" : "World"
  return <Title text={text} />
}
```

In the preceding example, a `Title` component accepts `text` as one of the props. An `App` component sends the `"Hello"` text to the `Title` component if the flag is `true`, otherwise, it sends the `"World"` text to `Title`.

Who sends the `flag` info to the `App` component? That will be the parent of `App`. This can easily be constructed to form a tree, where we have branches and sub-branches, and it reaches the leaves at the ends. Notice that this formation is done solely through the usage of props on each node (component).

Once a piece of info gets into a component, the prop binds its value to a local scope variable. From then on, it's the child's job to continue managing its local variable. It can be used pretty flexibly with one limitation. It's not expected to be changed! Or, if you ever change it, the change would not be reflected in the parent component. This behavior is the same as how we use a function with input arguments and its inner scope. The information passing is a one-way ticket.

So now comes a big question. What if we want to reflect the change to a parent component done by a child component? How can a one-way ticket get us the information back?

This is also done through a prop. As I mentioned, a prop can take any format, hence we can use a function prop:

```
const Child = ({ change }) => {
  const onChange = () => {
    change()
  }
  return <input onChange={onChange} />
}

const Parent = () => {
  const change = () => {
    console.log("child notify me")
  }
  return <Child change={change} />
}
```

In the preceding code, we sent a function defined in `Parent` through a `change` prop. Inside the `Child` component, when a user starts to type in any character to an `input` box, it fires an `onChange` event where we can invoke the `change` function. Whenever this happens, you will see the `child notify` me message in the `Parent` component.

Essentially, this technique is what we refer to as a callback in JavaScript. The parent provides a mechanism to notify that something has changed using a callback function. Once the callback function is created, it can be sent to any child to gain the ability of notification to the parent.

In a typical parent/child relationship in *React*, it's recommended that a prop value should not be changed by the child. Instead, it should be done through a function prop. When comparing *React* to other libraries, a "one-way" ticket is what we use to refer to this behavior. In the *React* community, we rarely use this word because this is the behavior designed at its birth.

Now that we know the definition of a function component and the role props play in building a component, let's take a look at how, in general, we write a function component.

Writing a function component

The function, representing a component, defines what to update on the screen. It returns a value composed of some *HTML*-like code. You should be quite familiar with elements such as `<ul>` and `<li>`; *React* also allows the addition of *JavaScript* expressions under these elements. When used together, it requires the *JavaScript* expression to be wrapped in a pair of brackets, { }. The job of this expression is to provide dynamic *HTML* content.

For instance, if we have a `text` variable and would like to display it, we could do the following:

```
const Title = () => {
  const text = "Hello World1"
  return <h1>{text}</h1>
}
```

Or, if the text is returned from a function, we can do the following:

```
const Title = () => {
  const fn = () => "Hello World"
  return <h1>{fn()}</h1>
}
```

We know that this *JavaScript* expression is filled in the location where the `children` prop is.

The children element does not have to be a single element; it can be an array of elements as well:

```
const Title = () => {
  const arr = ['Apple', 'Orange']
  return (
    <ul>
      {arr.map((v) => (
        <li>{v}</li>
      ))}
    </ul>
  )
}
```

It seems a bit complicated in the preceding code, so let's take a look at what the code tries to achieve by looking at the result first:

```
  return (
    <ul>
      {[<li>Apple</li>, <li>Orange</li>]}
    </ul>
  )
```

Basically, it wants to output two `li` elements. To get there, we create an array containing two elements with a *JavaScript* expression. Once it becomes a *JavaScript* expression wrapped in brackets, { }, anything in *JavaScript* can be refactored and programmed however we want. We can use `arr.map` to form this array:

```
  {['Apple', 'Orange'].map(v => (
    <li>{v}</li>
  ))}
```

Well done in code refactoring!

There are just so many different brackets shown in the preceding statement, including { }, [], and (). So, feel free to take a moment to understand what each pair does. It is hard to believe that one of the challenges of writing in *React* is brackets.

This is a good example that shows you that once things are wrapped in a *JavaScript* expression, they can be refactored as we would normally program. In this case, we can take the arr outside the function since arr is a constant that doesn't have to be defined inside the `Title` component:

```
const arr = ['Apple', 'Orange']

const Title = () => {
```

```
  return (
    <ul>
      {arr.map((v) => (
        <li>{v}</li>
      ))}
    </ul>
  )
}
```

Once you get a feel for using the JavaScript expression along with HTML-like code, sooner or later, you will develop your own programming style because underlying this exercise is the JavaScript language.

Now that you have gotten to know this process, let's code an example together.

Example of a function component

A site is made up of pages, where each page contains a sidebar, a header, a content area, and a footer. All of them can be modeled with components. The layout component can sit at the top of the tree. When you zoom in, you find its children inside with a sub-structure. Just like a spider's web (see *Figure 1.3*) the tree structure cascades down from the outer level into the inner level.

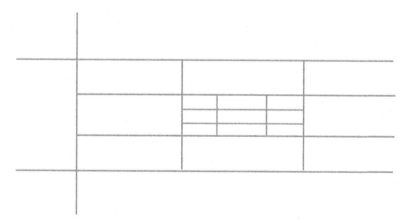

Figure 1.3 – Web application layout

As *UI* engineers, we focus on the design of each component. Moreover, we pay close attention to the relationship between components. We want to know whether Title is built inside the main content or the sidebar. We want to know whether a header needs to be shared by multiple pages. You'll start to develop the skill to navigate between components among a tree.

Say we want to display a list of navigation links at the top of the page. Each link can be disabled if required. For enabled ones, we can click to navigate to its corresponding *URL*. See *Figure 1.4*:

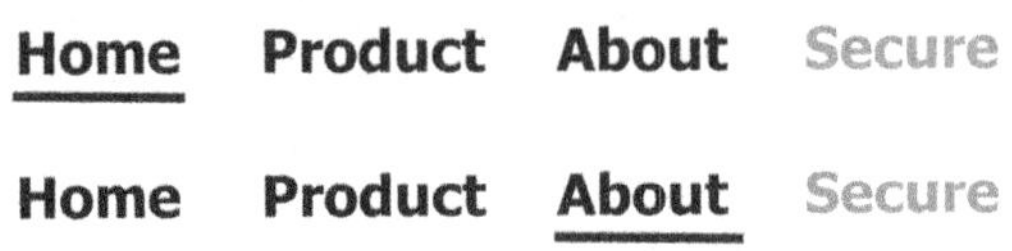

Home   **Product**   **About**   Secure

Home   **Product**   **About**   Secure

Figure 1.4 – Nav component

The navigation links can be predefined in an array of link objects:

```
const menus = [
  { key: 'home', label: 'Home' },
  { key: 'product', label: 'Product' },
  { key: 'about', label: 'About' },
  { key: 'secure', label: 'Secure', disabled: true },
]
```

In each of the preceding links, the `key` property provides an identifier, the `label` property specifies the displayed title, and the `disabled` property indicates whether the user is allowed to click on it or not.

We also want to display a line below the currently selected link. Based on these requirements, we come up with the implementation with `selected` and `items` props:

```
const Nav = ({ selected, items }) => {
  const isActive = item => item.key === selected
  const onClick = item => () => {
    window.location.href = item.url
  }
  return ...
}
```

In the preceding `Nav` component, the `items` prop holds the list of links, and the `selected` prop holds the current selected item's key. The job of the `Nav` component is to display the list:

```
  return (
    <ul>
      {items.map(item => (
        <li
          key={item.key}
          className={isActive(item) ? 'active' : ''}
        >
          <button
            disabled={item.disabled}
```

```
            onClick={onClick}
          >
            {item.label}
          </button>
        </li>
      ))}
    </ul>
  )
```

In the preceding `return` statement, `items` is iterated through one by one by following a loop and displaying links with a `ul`/`li` structure. Each link is displayed as a button supporting a `disabled` attribute. It also marks the link's *CSS* class as being `active` if it's the currently selected link.

Watch out for the `key` attribute for each item. This attribute is required for *React* to know the position of each `li` element among the lists. With the key provided as a unique identifier, *React* can quickly find the right element to perform the comparison and update the screen. `key` is a must-have attribute when returning an array of elements.

> **Playground – Nav Component**
>
> Feel free to play with the example online at `https://codepen.io/windmaomao/pen/porzQjV`.

Now we can display `Nav` with the following line. Voilà:

```
<Nav items={menus} selected="home" />
```

To make each menu item easy to develop and maintain, we can extract lines out to form a separate component:

```
const NavItem = ({
  label, active, disabled, onClick
}) => (
  <li className={active ? 'active' : ''}>
    <button disabled={disabled} onClick={onClick}>
      {label}
    </button>
  </li>
)
```

In the preceding code, a `NavItem` component is created to accept `label`, `active`, `disabled`, and `onClick` props. We don't need to overthink these prop names because they come in naturally, refactoring from the preceding `Nav` component. We can plug `NavItem` back to `Nav`:

```
const Nav = ({ selected, items }) => {
  const isActive = item => item.key === selected
  const onClick = item => () => {
    window.location.href = item.url
  }

  return (
    <ul>
      {items.map(item => (
        <NavItem
          key={item.key}
          label={item.label}
          disabled={item.disabled}
          active={isActive(item)}
          onClick={onClick(item)}
        />
      ))}
    </ul>
  )
}
```

This refactoring exercise is quite common and effective. This way, both `Nav` and `NavItem` components become easier to maintain in the future.

Summary

In this chapter, we first went over the history of UI components by looking at four libraries – *jQuery*, *Angular*, *React*, and *LitElement* – to get an idea of having a component and how components are put together to build an application. Then, we learned what a function component is, with an introduction to its props and parent/child relationship. We then learned how to write a function component in general, and finally, we built a `Nav` component step by step.

In the next chapter, we will craft a state of the function component from scratch and see how actions can benefit from it.

Questions and answers

Here are some questions and answers to refresh your knowledge:

1. What is a function component?

    A function component is a function taking props as its input argument and returning elements. For an App component, we can display it by using its instance form, <App />. To build an application, it's about putting a component under another component as a child and refining this process until we end up with a tree of components.

2. How do you write a function component?

    The way to become adept at writing function components is quite similar to writing functions. Ask yourself what the props specification of the component is and what is returned for display. In a typical application, half of the components are designed for business requirements, but the other half normally comes from code refactoring. A study of **Functional Programming** (**FP**) can generally benefit you and take your UI skills to the next level.

Appendix

Appendix A – How many component types does React support?

In the published *React* documentation, it supports two component types. One is a function component, and another one is a class component. *React* supported the class component from the beginning:

```
class ClassComponent extends React.Component {
  render() {
    const { name } = this.props;
    return <h1>Hello, { name }</h1>;
  }
}
```

Although the render function of a class component looks quite similar to what a function component returns and, most of the time, we can convert them in between, the class and function components are treated differently inside the *React* update process. Therefore, this book intentionally avoids mentioning the class component so as not to confuse any newcomer to *React*.

In general, a function component can be written shorter and simpler, and it's also easier in terms of development and testing because it has plain inputs and outputs. Also, it doesn't have the `this` keyword, which can intimidate new developers or sometimes even senior developers. However, the downside of using a function component is that it's relatively new to the programming world, and there's also a mentality shift from **Object-Oriented Programming (OOP)** to **Functional Programming (FP)**, which can consume you if you are not prepared. Not to mention, being new means there can be different approaches that we need to learn and absorb before we can address the old problems.

Other than the class and function components, internally, *React* actually supports more component types, as in the following example:

```
import { memo } from 'react'

const Title = memo(() => <h1>Hello</h1>)
const App = () => <Title />
```

When the `memo` function is applied to the `Title` component, it creates a component with a component type, `MemoComponent`. We don't need to go into the details of these component types, but just know that each component type gets its own update algorithm when updated to the screen.

2
Crafting States in Functions

In the previous chapter, we learned how to write function components in *React*. In this chapter, we will craft a special variable called a state in the function components.

We will see what benefits a state can bring us, including requesting a new update, making a variable persistent, listening to a value change, as well as performing tasks upon the mount. We will also see an example of applying a state to a single-page application. In the end, we will look closely at what role the states play within the *UI*.

We will cover the following topics in this chapter:

- Crafting a state in a function component
- Applying states to single-page applications
- How states work with UIs
- Questions and answers

Technical requirements

Before beginning, I would like you to know about the timeline sketch:

```
|--x---x---x-x--x--x------> user event
```

The timeline sketch is a unique illustrative chart type that displays a series of events during a period. The left bar (|) stands for the time origin, representing the first update. The horizontal dash (-) moves with the time from left to right with an arrow > at the end. Each letter or number, such as x , indicates one event that happened in this timeline. In this book, we will use the timeline sketch to better understand a situation when multiple things happen simultaneously along the timeline.

Crafting a state in a function component

When you visit a typical web page, it asks for your username and password. After you log in, it displays the content of what the website provides, such as blogs, tweets, or videos, in a chronological order. You can vote on them and put your comments there – a very typical web experience these days.

When you surf a website like that as a user, you don't put too much thought into how any of the actions are implemented, nor do you care about the order in which each is fired. However, when it comes to building the site yourself, each action and the time at which each gets fired starts to become important.

An action handler fires when a user clicks a button, hovers over an icon, scrolls down a paragraph, types on the keyboard, and so on. A typical relationship between a user event and an action handler is illustrated in the following:

```
|--x---x---x-x--x--x------> user event
|--a---a---a-a--a--a------> action handler
```

In the preceding sketch, basically, an x in the user event series is followed by an a in the user event series. Based on this, we can start to handle a user action.

Let's turn ourselves to a "Hello World" `Title` component with a button inside. Each time we click the button, a counter gets incremented by one and appended after **Hello World+**, as shown in *Figure 2.1*:

Figure 2.1 – Hello World with no state

To implement that, we start with a `count` variable to store a number initialized as `0`:

```
function Title() {
  let count = 0
  const onClick = () => {
    count = count + 1
  }
  return (
    <>
      <button onClick={onClick}>+</button>
      <h1>Hello World+{count}</h1>
    </>
  )
}
```

In the preceding `Title` component, the response to the user click is implemented via a React event handler, `onClick`, wired to a `button` element.

A *React* event handler is written slightly differently from a *DOM* event handler. You can tell from the `onClick` camel case name, rather than the `onclick` lowercase name. A *React* event is a synthetic event that is a cross-browser wrapper around the browser native event. In this book, we expect them to behave in exactly the same way.

Thanks to the *JavaScript* closure, we can directly access any component variable inside the event handler. The `count` variable does not need to be passed into `onClick` as a function input argument to be accessed.

If we run the code, we'd expect the title to display **Hello World+1** after we click the button. But to our surprise, no matter how many times we clicked the button, it still displayed **Hello World+0**. To figure out what happened, let's add `console.log` to two locations.

One is placed before `count = count + 1` to confirm what the `count` is after incrementation. Another one is placed before the `return` statement to confirm what the updated `count` is when the `Title` component is updated. They are marked at ① and ② in the following code:

```
function Title() {
  let count = 0
  const onClick = () => {
    console.log('clicked', count)      ①
    count = count + 1
  }
  console.log('updated', count)      ②
  return ...
}
```

With these two logs placed, we can rerun the code and generate a new timeline sketch:

```
|----0--1-2--3-4----5------> clicked   ①
0-------------------------> updated    ②
```

From the preceding printout, a `clicked` series at ① showed the `count` number when the button was clicked, and it was clicked six times. Let's turn to another log, the `updated` series at ②; the `count` value got updated once as 0, which explains why the display remained as `Hello World+0`.

The `updated` series with only one printout at the very beginning indicates that there weren't any more updates after the first one. This is quite a discovery. If there were no more updates, how can we expect to see a change on the screen?

> **Playground – No State**
>
> Feel free to play with this example online at `https://codepen.io/windmaomao/pen/jOLNXzO`.

As you might already realize, we need to request a new update after the click.

Requesting a new update

To make an update, for the time being, we can borrow the `render` function provided by *React*, as we have already used it to update the `rootEl` element:

```
ReactDOM.render(<Title />, rootEl)
```

Let's take a minute to see how *React* updates the screen in general (see *Figure 2.2*). The detail involving updates can be quite complex; for now, let's treat it as a black box. We will get into more details later in the book:

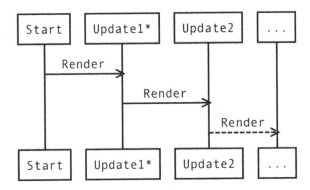

Figure 2.2 – React update

When an app starts, it lands on an update. This first update is a bit special. Because all the DOM elements need to be created, we refer to this update as a mount.

What's important to know is that a new update wouldn't arrive unless it's requested, just as we invoke a `render` function. When people first come to React, they might think it works as a game engine.

For instance, a game engine would request a new update every 1/60 second behind the scenes. But *React* does not do that! Instead, the developer should get precise control of when a new update is requested. And most of the time, the frequency is a lot lower than 1/60 second, and it's more or less driven by how fast a user acts on the website.

So with this, to bring the new `count` to the screen, another update needs to be requested manually; if we borrow the `render`, we can use it after the `count` is incremented:

```
const onClick = () => {
  console.log('clicked', count)          ①
  count = count + 1
  ReactDOM.render(<Title />, rootEl)
}
```

If we run the preceding code with the addition of `render`, the timeline sketch changes to the following:

```
|----0--0-0--0-0----0------> clicked   ①
0----0--0-0--0-0----0------> updated   ②
```

To our surprise, all numbers displayed were 0. Looking at the `updated` series at ②, note we got seven printouts, which means we got six more updates on top of the first update. However, the `clicked` series at ① shows that the `count` value changed to 0 and stopped to increment any more. Weird?!

How could the `count` value be stuck at 0? Something must happen to the new update, but the `render` function can't be the one that resets the `count` value back to 0, can it?

It's important to know that upon the `render` function being called and a function component being updated, the function that defines the component gets invoked, as shown in *Figure 2.3*:

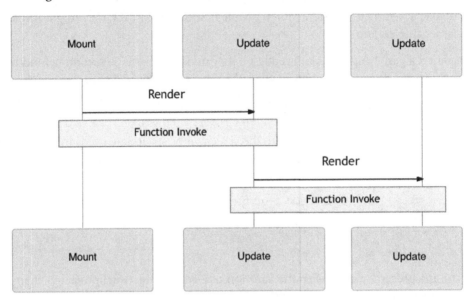

Figure 2.3 – React render for a function component

With this knowledge, let's take a look at the `Title` function again:

```
const Title = () => {
  let count = 0
  // omitting the onClick statement
  console.log('updated', count)          ②
  // omitting the return statement
}
```

In the preceding code, we intentionally omit the `onClick` and `return` statements to make the code a bit cleaner. What was left became a `let count = 0` declaration statement. During each update, the `Title` function gets invoked, thus creating a new scope of the function. Inside this scope, there's a variable `count` value created locally to hold a 0 number. So this code doesn't seem to do much.

It's not too difficult to see now why the `count` value remains at 0, isn't it? It doesn't really matter if we have added the increment logic onClick or `return` statement. Upon each update, the entire function scope gets a new one with a `count` value declared and set to 0. That explains why the `console.log` statement followed a printed 0.

This is actually the reason why a function component was named as a stateless function when it was introduced to *React* initially. "Stateless" refers to the fact that a function component can't carry or share a value to another update. In a simple word, the function reruns in each update with the same output.

Okay, now we understand the problem. So, it makes us consider saving the `count` value somewhere and making it persistent for another update.

Making a value persistent

JavaScript supports a function scope: Variables defined inside a function cannot be accessed from anywhere outside the function, thus each function has its own scope. If you invoke a function multiple times, there'll be multiple scopes. But no matter how many times we invoke it, it wouldn't create a different output, such as what happened in the movie *Groundhog Day*.

> **Note**
>
> The movie *Groundhog Day* is a 1993 fantasy comedy film, where Phil wakes up every day to find he experiences the previous day's events repeating exactly and believes he is experiencing déjà vu.

For our `count` value, we can visualize what happened with the two updates in two different scopes in *Figure 2.4*:

Figure 2.4 – Two function scopes for the two updates

Luckily, *JavaScript* supports a function scope in a way that it can access all variables defined inside the scope in which it is defined. In our case, if a variable is defined outside of the `Title` function, we can access this variable inside the `Title` functions, as this value is shared now between multiple `Title` functions.

The easiest way of sharing is to create a global variable because the global variable lives in the most outer scope of the *JavaScript* code, thus it can be accessed inside any function.

> **Note**
> Don't be intimidated by a global variable used in this chapter. In *Chapter 3, Hooking into React*, we will refine this approach and see how *React* defines the variable in a better location.

This way, each local count value can set/get this global count value, as shown in *Figure 2.5*:

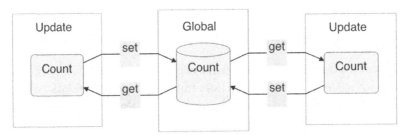

Figure 2.5 – A shared value among the two updates

Okay, with this new global variable idea, let's see whether we can break out of our *Groundhog Day* situation:

```
let m = undefined
function _getM(initialValue) {
  if (m === undefined) {
    m = initialValue
  }
  return m
}
function _setM(value) {
  m = value
  ReactDOM.render(<Title />, rootEl)
}
```

In the preceding code, a global variable, m, is allocated, and it comes with _getM getter and _setM setter methods. The _getM function returns the value but sets the initial value for the first time. The _setM function sets the value and requests a new update. Let's apply _getM and _setM to our Title component:

```
function Title() {
  let count = _getM(0)
  const onClick = () => {
```

```
    console.log('clicked', count)        ①
    count = count + 1
    _setM(count)
  }
  console.log('updated', count)          ②
  return ...
}
```

Inside the preceding amended `Title` component, all `count` variables across updates are linked with the help of `_getM` and `_setM`. If we rerun the code, we can see the following timeline sketch:

```
|----0--1-2--3-4----5------> clicked   ①
0----1--2-3--4-5----6------> updated   ②
```

Wow! The screen changes to `Hello World+1` upon the first click and increments further upon more clicks, as shown in Figure 2.6:

Figure 2.6 – Hello World counter using a state

Congratulations! You just crafted a state inside a function component.

> **Playground – Count State**
>
> Feel free to play with this example online at `https://codepen.io/windmaomao/pen/KKvPJdg`.

The word "state" refers to the fact that it's persisted for all updates. For our convenience, we also change the state and request a new update afterward to reflect the change to the screen.

So, now we know how to handle a user action with a state. Let's see whether we can expand this idea further to support multiple states instead of one state.

Support multiple states

It's great that we can establish a state persistent within a function component. But we want more states like that. An app normally contains lots of buttons, switches, and actionable items; each requires a state to be persistent. So, it's a must-have to support multiple states in the same app.

So, say we need two buttons and each needs to be driven by a state. Let's extend what we have learned from a single state:

```
const Title = () => {
  let countH = _getM(0)
  let countW = _getM(0)
  const onClickH = () => {
    countH = countH + 1
    _setM(countH)
  }
  const onClickW = () => {
    countW = countW + 1
    _setM(countW)
  }
  return (
    <>
      <button onClick={onClickH}>+</button>
      <h1>Hello+{countH}</h1>
      <button onClick={onClickW}>+</button>
      <h1>World+{countW}</h1>
    </>
  )
}
```

In the preceding code, we first created two buttons, one with a **Hello** label and one with a **World** label, and each have their separate event handler, onClickH and onClickW respectively. Also, we applied _getM and _setM to both of them, and installed a couple of logs to help the debug, as shown in the following timeline sketch:

```
|----0--1-2----------------> clickedH
|------------3-4----5------> clickedW
0----1--2-3--4-5----6------> updatedH
0----1--2-3--4-5----6------> updatedW
```

From the preceding sketch, we clicked the **Hello** button three times and then clicked the **World** button three times. The numbers corresponding to both buttons all updated upon clicking, as shown in the updatedH and updatedW series. However, the two series seem to be inseparable and in sync, meaning clicking one button would increment both values at the same time!

Playground – Linked States

Feel free to play with this example online at https://codepen.io/ windmaomao/pen/qBXWgay.

Okay, it's not too difficult to find out that we actually made a mistake by wiring the same state to both buttons; no wonder they updated at the same time:

```
let countH = _getM(0)
let countW = _getM(0)
```

Although this is not what we wanted to achieve, it's interesting to see that a state is shared by two buttons. Visually, we linked two buttons; clicking one triggers the click on another.

So, what can we do if we want to have two separate states with each controlling one button? Well, we can just add another state. This time, we want to be a bit more generic in using a list to hold any number of states.

There are lots of ways to keep track of a list of values in *JavaScript*; one of the ways is to use a key/value pair, as in an object:

```
let states = {}

function _getM2(initialValue, key) {
  if (states[key] === undefined) {
    states[key] = initialValue
  }
  return states[key]
}
function _setM2(v, key) {
  states[key] = v
  ReactDOM.render(<Title />, rootEl)
}
```

In the preceding code, we declare a `states` object to store all state values. The `_getM2` and `_setM2` functions are almost similar to the single-value version we crafted earlier, except this time we store each state under `states[key]` instead of m, thus a `key` is needed to identify each state. With this change, let's amend the `Title` component:

```
function Title() {
  let countH = _getM2(0, 'H')
  let countW = _getM2(0, 'W')
  const onClickH = () => {
    console.log('clickedH', countH)
    countH = countH + 1
    _setM2(countH, 'H')
  }
  const onClickW = () => {
    console.log('clickedW', countW)
    countW = countW + 1
    _setM2(countW, 'W')
```

```
    }
    console.log('updatedH', countH)
    console.log('updatedW', countW)
    return ...
}
```

In the preceding amended version, we give a key to two states as H and W. We need this key for both set and get when a state is involved. Rerun the code and take a look at the timeline sketch:

```
|----0--1-2---------------> clickedH
|------------0-1----2------> clickedW
0----1--2-3--3-3----3------> updatedH
0----0--0-0--1-2----3------> updatedW
```

Once again, we clicked the **Hello** button three times and **World** button three times in a row. The numbers on both buttons all updated upon clicking, but this time, countH and countW are actually incremented separately, as you can see in the updatedH and updatedW series.

After the first three clicks on the **Hello** button, countH stays at 3 when we click on the **World** button. This is what we want to have, two separate states, as shown in *Figure 2.7*:

Figure 2.7 – Hello and World buttons with two states

> **Playground – Multiple States**
>
> Feel free to play with this example online at https://codepen.io/ windmaomao/pen/dyzbaVr.

The state we crafted so far requests a new update. This is a very good use of persistency in a function component; since being persistent is actually quite a generic feature, it should be utilized for many different purposes. So, what other things can we do with it? Let's take a look at another usage of a state.

Listen to a value change

You might wonder why we need to listen to a value change. Aren't the developers the ones who control the change of a value? As in the previous example, we use the event handler to change a counter. We know in this case exactly when the value gets changed.

That's true for this case, but there are other cases. You might send a value into a child component via a prop, or there might be two components that touch a value at the same time. In either of these cases, you can lose track of the moment when the value is changed, but you still want to perform an action upon the value change. This means that you want to have the ability to listen to a value change. Let's set up one example to demonstrate this.

Say in our **Hello World** button example that for any count change, we want to know whether this value has recently been changed:

```
function Changed({ count }) {
  let flag = 'N'
  return <span>{flag}</span>
}
```

In the preceding Changed component, there's a count prop that is sent from its parent, say any of the **Hello** or **World** buttons that we built earlier. We want to display Y or N, depending on whether the count value has changed. We can use this Changed component in the Title component:

```
function Title() {
  ...
  return (
    <>
      <button onClick={onClickH}>+</button>
      <h1>Hello+{countH}</h1>
      <Changed count={countH} />
      <button onClick={onClickW}>+</button>
      <h1>World+{countW}</h1>
    </>
  )
}
```

Note that in the preceding code, we add the Changed component between two buttons, and what we want to see is the Changed component display Y when we click the **Hello** button, and the Changed component display N when we click on the **World** button. Essentially, we want to know whether the change is coming from the **Hello** button or not. But when we ran the code, here's what we got in the timeline sketch:

```
0----1--2-3--3-3----3------> updatedH
0----0--0-0--1-2----3------> updatedW
N----N--N-N--N-N----N------> Changed flag
```

From the preceding sketch, you can see that no matter which button is clicked, the flag in the Changed flag series displayed N. This comes as no surprise, since you might have already noticed that the flag inside the Changed component is fixed at N, so it wouldn't work the way we wanted. But the reason we wrote N there is because we don't know what to write there to flip the flag.

When the **Hello** button gets clicked three times, the countH value, as in the updatedH series, increments to 3. Similarly, when the **World** button gets the next three clicks, the countW value, as in the updatedW series, increments to 3. However, note that as the countW value increments, the countH value also gets printed out; see 3-3-3 in the updatedH series.

This indicates that for each update, every element under the return statement gets updated. Either countW or countH changes; it comes to a new update of the Title component, thus updating all button and h1 elements. The same applies to the Changed component; whichever button changes, the Changed function gets invoked. Therefore, we can't tell whether the update to the Changed component is due to the **Hello** button or the **World** button.

If we print out the count prop under the Changed component, it will look the same as in the updatedH series:

```
0----1--2-3--3-3----3------> count
```

Looking at the preceding count value, in order to come up with the changed flag for whether it changes from the previous value, we need to make a value persistent again – in this case, to get hold of the previous value. For example, 0 to 1 is a change, but 3 to 3 isn't.

Okay, to put this idea to work, let's borrow the state approach but this time apply it to a prev value:

```
let prev
function _onM(callback, value) {
  if (value === prev) return
  callback()
  prev = value
}
```

In the preceding code, we allocated a `prev` global variable and a `_onM` utility function. The `onM` function is designed to run a `callback` function when the `value` changes. It first checks whether the `value` is equal to the `prev` value. It returns if there's no change. But if there is, the `callback` function is then invoked, and the current `value` replaces the `prev` value. Let's apply this `_onM` function to the `Changed` component:

```
function Changed({ count }) {
  let flag = 'N'
  _onM(() => { flag = 'Y' }, count)
  return <span>{flag}</span>
}
```

With the preceding change, we rerun the code and take a look at the updated timeline sketch:

```
0----1--2-3--3-3----3------> updatedH
0----0--0-0--1-2----3------> updatedW
Y----Y--Y-Y--N-N----N------> Changed flag
```

Interestingly enough, when we clicked the **Hello** button this time, it displayed Y, and when we clicked the **World** button afterward, it changed to N, as shown in *Figure 2.8*:

Figure 2.8 – Listen to value change

Wonderful! Also, notice the first Y at the mount in the `Changed flag` series, which is when `countH` changes from `undefined` to `0`. Please make a note here; we'll talk about it in the next section.

> **Playground – Listening to State Change**
>
> Feel free to play with this example online at `https://codepen.io/windmaomao/pen/MWvgxLR`.

Being able to listen to a value change is quite useful because it provides us with another way to perform tasks. Without it, we have to rely on an event handler, which is mostly driven by user actions. With `_onM`, we can perform a task upon a value change, which can come out of any other process.

When listening to a value change, there exists a moment at the mount. This means that we can perform a task at the mount because of it. Let's take a look at it more closely.

Performing a task at the mount

Components mount and un-mount as things show up and disappear based on the business requirement. At the mount, it's common to want to perform a task such as initializing some variables, calculating some formulas, or fetching an *API* to get some resources over the internet. Let's use an *API* call as an example.

Say a `count` value needs to be fetched from an online service called `/giveMeANumber`. When this fetch returns successfully, we would like to reflect the change to the screen:

```
fetch('/giveMeANumber').then(res => {
  ReactDOM.render(<Title />, rootEl)
})
```

The preceding code is what we'd like to do; however, we run into a technical issue right away. Though a new update can be requested, how can we send the returned data to the `Title` component?

Maybe we can set up a prop on the `Title` component to send it in. However, doing that would require us to change the component interface. Since we already have had states crafted to issue a new update, let's try that approach:

```
fetch('./giveMeANumber').then(res => {
  _setM(res.data)
})
function Title() => {
  const count = _getM("")
  return <h1>{count}</h1>
}
```

In the preceding code, by using `_setM` after the fetch returns, we can update a state with the received `res.data` and request a new update afterward. The new update invokes `Title` and reads the latest `count` from the state via `_getM`.

Currently, we define the `fetch` function parallel to the `Title` component, but this is not the right location since we want to fetch only at the mount. To fix that, we can listen to the mount, as we have learned in the previous section:

```
_onM(() => { ... }, 0)
```

Using the preceding line, we can listen for a mount moment. Note that we watched a constant 0 instead of any variable. During the mount, the value that _onM listens to changes from undefined to 0, but for other future updates, the value stays at 0; therefore, the . . . callback gets invoked only once at the mount. Let's write fetch inside this callback:

```
function Title() => {
  const count = _getM(0)
  _onM(() => {
    fetch('./giveMeANumber').then(res => {
      _setM(res.data)
    })
  }, 0)
  console.log('u')
  return <h1>{count}</h1>
}
```

If we run the preceding code, the timeline sketch should generate the following:

```
u-----u-------------------> log
```

At the mount of the Title component, the count state is set to be 0 initially. A fetch function is performed right away, depicted as the first u in the preceding updates series. Only when fetch returns successfully does the count state get updated to a new value and refreshed to the screen. The new update is depicted as the second u in the updates series.

> **Playground – Task at Mount**
>
> Feel free to play with this example online at https://codepen.io/windmaomao/pen/PoKobVZ.

Between the first and the second update, that's how long it takes for the API to finish. The relationship between the API, the state, and two updates is illustrated in *Figure 2.9*. Essentially, after the API returns, it communicates to the shared state where the new update picks up later:

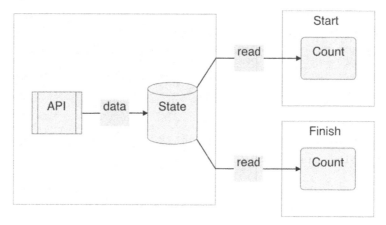

Figure 2.9 – Fetch API within the stateful component

Now that we have crafted a state, and also seen how flexible a state can be used to either make a new update or listen to a value change, let's get hands-on and apply what we have learned to an app.

Applying states to single-page application

We want to continue what we started in the previous chapter in building a single-page application. We couldn't finish it back then because we lacked a way to switch to a different page other than the home page. We had put together a Nav component:

```
const Nav = ({ items, selected }) => { ... }
```

Given a list of pages, the Nav component displays them as links to navigate. The currently selected page needs to be provided as well. Now that we know how to define a state, let's use it to keep track of the selected page:

```
const App = () => {
  const selected = _getM("home")
  return (
    <div>
      <Nav
        items={menus}
        selected={selected}
        onSelect={_setM}
```

```
        / >
        ...
    </div>
  )
}
```

In the preceding `App` component, we used a state for `selected` to hold the `home` key initially, which is then passed into the `Nav` component. To allow the state to be updated after a user click, we need to modify `Nav` by adding the support of an `onSelect` callback function:

```
const Nav = ({ items, selected, onSelect }) => {
  const isActive = item => item.key === selected
  const onClick = item => () => {
    onSelect(item.key)
  }
  ...
}
```

In the preceding amended `Nav` component, an `onSelect` prop is passed so that after `onClick`, the parent `App` component can be notified to update the `selected` page via the `_setM` function.

To confirm that the user does reach a different page, based on the current selected page, we can use a `Route` component to switch between page content:

```
const Route = ({ selected }) => {
    return (
      <div>
      {selected === 'home' && <Home />}
      {selected === 'product' && <Product />}
    </div>
    )
}
```

What the preceding `Route` component does is display the page content based on the `selected` page. Note that it uses a `&&` symbol, which is a common line in *React* code. It's equivalent to the following:

```
{selected === 'home' ? <Home /> : false}
```

If the condition matches on the left part, it returns `<Home />`; otherwise, it returns `false`. And according to *React*, any `true`, `false`, `null`, or `undefined` values are all valid elements, but when updated, they all get ignored without being displayed. Essentially, if the left part condition doesn't meet, it displays nothing.

Putting the `Nav` and `Route` components together, we can amend the `App` component:

```
const Home = () => <h1>Home page</h1>
const Product = () => <h1>Product page</h1>
const App = () => {
  const selected = _getM("home")
  return (
    <div>
      <Nav
        items={menus}
        selected={selected}
        onSelect={_setM}
      />
      <Routes selected={selected} />
    </div>
  )
}
```

Finally, we got two pages working, as shown in *Figure 2.10*! If you click the **Product** link, it'll land on the product page:

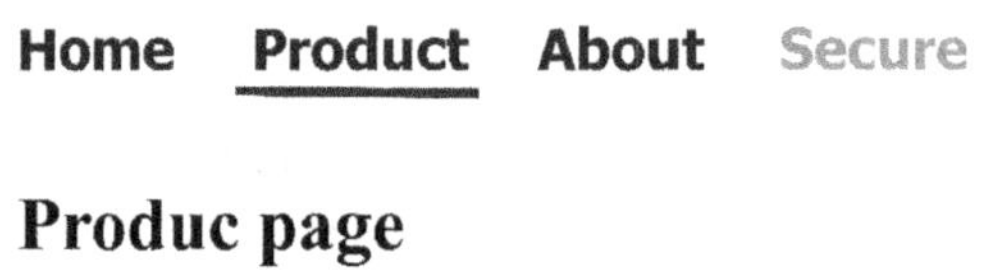

Home   Product   About   Secure

Produc page

Figure 2.10 – A single-page application using a state

To recap, the `App` component defines a `selected` state to hold the currently `selected` page. The `Nav` component is used to display all the links and allow it to choose a different page by clicking on the link. The `Route` component is used to display a page based on the `selected` state. Essentially, based on this setup, adding more pages is just a matter of adding new components under the `Route` component.

> **Playground – Single-Page Application**
>
> Feel free to play with this example online at `https://codepen.io/windmaomao/pen/PoKoWPG`.

Before we end this chapter, let's take a minute to look at how exactly a state drives the UI under *React*.

How states work with UI

With the introduction of state to the function component, we sometimes can get dizzy by the roles that it plays. We will use three components to elaborate, as shown in *Figure 2.11*:

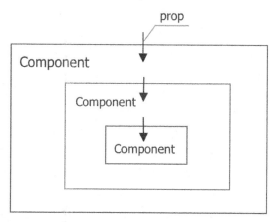

Figure 2.11 – Props in components

We have three components depicted in solid boxes. The outer component contains the middle one as a child, and the middle one contains the inner one as a child. Props, depicted as arrow lines crossing the boundary of a solid box, pass values from a parent to a child component.

React is a state machine. For a given fixed set of variables, it paints the screen the same way. With props, this is quite straightforward since each component is solely determined by its props. Now, let's add the states to the picture, as shown in *Figure 2.12*. States, depicted as a symbol with a circle and a dot, are defined inside each component:

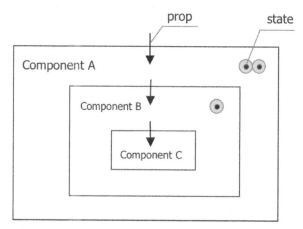

Figure 2.12 – States and props in components

Taking the **C** inner component first, it doesn't have any state defined. So, it's still determined by its props.

The **B** middle component has one state defined. With a fixed set of its props, the screen corresponding to the component still can vary because this state can take a different value on each update.

The **A** outer component has two states defined. Similarly, with all its props fixed, the screen corresponding to it can still vary. The variation can come from any of its two states, and it can come from the state of the **B** component as well because the states of the parent and the child can work independently upon updates.

Therefore, we can conclude that to get the screen painted for the **A** component, we need to fix all props and states within itself and all its child components underneath. This is not a mathematical theory, but given the states from multiple components, this observation is apparent.

In short, props and states now both serve as the input of the component. The states can be especially vibrant since their values can be, but are not always, wired with an external system. The external system can be browser events or the *API* fetch, or anything else. Because a state can send to a child component via a prop, the effect of the state can cascade down deep into the app tree quickly.

Summary

In this chapter, we started to craft a new thing called a state inside the function component. The state is persistent across updates and can be used to request a new update, listen to a value change, as well as perform a task at the mount. Later, we applied the state we developed to a single-page application to draft a simplified Nav with a route system. In the end, we briefly studied how states work for *UI* under *React*.

In the next chapter, we will introduce you to what a React hook is and how this persistent state is designed under the *React* engine.

Questions and answers

Here are some questions and answers to refresh your knowledge:

1. What is a state?

    For a function component, a state is a value created to be persistent during the life of the component. From each update, including the mount, this value can be accessed from inside a function.

2. What are the usages of states?

   If a task can't be done within one update, that is the time we can think of using a state to reference a memory that can be accessed in multiple updates. We normally use a state to request a new update, listen to a value change, as well as perform a task at the mount. But the states can be very versatile.

3. What does a state do to the UI?

   To determine the screen corresponding to a component, we need to know its states as well as its props. While the props are passively defined on the component interface, the states are defined inside the component to actively refine its behavior. Apps built with states can change with time, driven by either user interactions or any other external processes.

3
Hooking into React

In the previous chapter, we learned to perform actions inside a function component with our crafted states. In this chapter, we will go through the challenges we face in creating a good state solution, and then see how *React* builds the solution with the underlying Hook. We will then introduce what a hook is and get to know it, as well as its calling order, and learn how to avoid running into conditional hook issues in real applications. The chapter also includes two bonus topics in the *Appendix* section, *React Fiber* and *Current and WorkInProgress Scenes*.

We will cover the following topics in this chapter:

- Creating good state solution
- Introducing a React Hook
- What is a hook?
- Questions and answers
- Appendix

Creating a good state solution

States are quite capable. A component without states is like a function without variables. It would lack capabilities of reasoning. A piece of UI logic relies on states to work upon continuous interactions from users.

We built a custom state in the previous chapter as follows:

```
let states = {}
function _getM2(initialValue, key) {
  if (states[key] === undefined) {
    states[key] = initialValue
  }
  return states[key]
}
function _setM2(v, key) {
  states[key] = v
  ReactDOM.render(<Title />, rootEl)
}
```

Though this approach works, there are a few problems we need to address before we can be seriously considered using it with *React*. We'll mention these problems one by one as follows.

The location where the states are allocated is the first major problem:

```
let states = {}
```

The preceding `states` variable is allocated as a global variable, but normally we'd be first interested in states specific to a component. In other words, we need to find a place to define local states.

The second problem of using states is the unique key to identify each of them:

```
const a = _getM2(0, 'comp_a')
```

As in the preceding state usage, after we name the state `comp_a`, we have to carry this key for any actions involving this state. In a typical application, we could have lots of states like that; if each has to be defined with a unique string, we would have to come up with a lot of unique names. It would be quite some work to keep track of all the used names, not to mention that the variable holding the state inside the function component already has a name, `a`. It's a bit cumbersome to have both the variable name and key string.

Other than these two major problems, there are other minor things we need to consider. In demonstrating the usage of the state, we render the `Title` component when we need to request a new update:

```
ReactDOM.render(<Title />, rootEl)
```

Explicitly knowing which component we need to update for each action we perform can be a challenge to developers. It would be better if the engine can help us here to hide away this detail by figuring out what the components are that need to be updated. This is exactly what *React* does best; we should wire it with the engine to perform the right update. Last but not least, we know that the states can be used for different purposes since the underlying concept is a persistency mechanism. If done properly, we should be able to create some sort of infrastructure upon which we can add additional functionalities.

The preceding is a list of issues that a good state solution should consider. With these in mind, let's take a look at how *React* approaches this state problem.

Introducing a React Hook

The state is mostly local to a component, at least as far as this book is mostly concerned. The natural place for storage would be under a component instance because a component in *React* defines a piece of UI. So, where is the component instance of a function component in *React* stored?

It turns out that a component isn't the smallest unit in *React*. There's a more granular structure called fiber, which is used to represent a piece of element. A fiber performs all the tasks for this element. The element can be as simple as `h1`, `div` elements, or it can be an artificial element that does things differently. For instance, a "fragment" element can group other elements without displaying itself, or a "memo" element can remember all the elements from the last update.

Actually, a function component is one of the artificial elements that a fiber represents. What a function component does is allow us to define what elements it can display, so whenever it's invoked, it can figure out what DOM elements the screen needs to update. You can find more information in *Appendix A – React Fiber* at the end of this chapter.

So, now we find the unit for a component instance; that's exactly where *React* decides to store states. *React* stores them under a memoizedState property using a Hook structure, as shown in *Figure 3.1*:

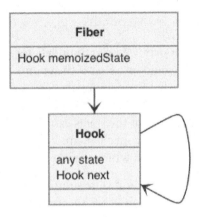

Figure 3.1 – Hooks under a fiber

The Hook we introduce here is a structure (or a class) to hold a state. This is not exactly the *React* hook (function) we will introduce later. Unfortunately, *React* uses the same word at both places. To distinguish them, we intentionally use *Hook* (with an uppercase *H*) for the structure and *hook* (with a lowercase *h*) for the function.

The main functionality of a Hook structure is to hold a single state under the state property. Instead of having multiple states in an array (or an object), multiple states are linked together using a linked list, as shown in *Figure 3.2*. One Hook points to another one via its next property. When it reaches the end of the list, the next property of the last Hook is set to be null. This is how a typical linked list works in programming. The first Hook, if any, is stored under the memoizedState of the fiber; this way, a fiber can find all Hooks following the first one.

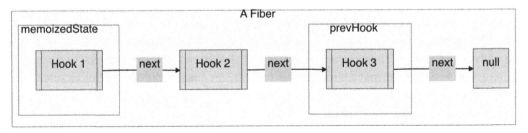

Figure 3.2 – Hooks in a Linked List

A fiber needs to be updated for the engine to know whether there is any change to the screen. In the update function, this is where the Hook gets initialized. So next, let's take a look at the update function.

Updating a function component

React updates a function component through an `updateFunctionComponent` function. The input arguments accept a `Component` function and its `props` input:

```
let updatingFiber = ...
function updateFunctionComponent(Component, props) {
  prevHook = null
  let children = Component(props)
  ...
}
```

The main job of the update function is to invoke `Component(props)` to know the new `children` element. Taking a `Title` component as an example, when it gets to be updated, the `updateFunctionComponent` function invokes `Title()`. With that, the engine compares the element returned and what's on the screen and commits the difference.

There are two global variables defined in the preceding update function. They are quite easy to follow. `updatingFiber` represents the current fiber that is under update by the engine, and `prevHook` points to the previously worked Hook for this fiber. Before the component is invoked, `updatingFiber` is populated by the engine, such as `Title`, and `prevHook` is set to be `null`.

The first time a component is updated, as in a mount, is when the first Hook for this fiber is created.

Creating a Hook at the mount

To mount a Hook under the currently updating fiber, *React* creates a new Hook object and appends it to the linked list:

```
function mountHook() {
  const Hook = {
    state: null
    next: null
  }
  if (prevHook === null) {
    updatingFiber.memoizedState = Hook
    prevHook = Hook
```

```
  } else {
    prevHook.next = Hook
    prevHook = prevHook.next
  }
  return Hook
}
```

In the preceding mountHook function, an empty Hook object is allocated first with both state and next set to null. If it's the first Hook to the fiber, as preHook is null, it gets stored under memoizedState of the fiber. Otherwise, it gets appended to the previous Hook's next property. After that, the allocated Hook is returned.

Obtaining a Hook at the update

In any other update after the mount, we can access Hooks that *React* created at the mount:

```
function updateHook() {
  var Hook
  if (prevHook === null) {
    Hook = updatingFiber.memoizedState
  } else {
    Hook = prevHook.next
  }
  prevHook = Hook
  return Hook
}
```

In the preceding updateHook function, a Hook object is obtained by looking for the first memoizedState Hook under the fiber. After the first Hook, it is obtained by following the next property of prevHook. *React* also keeps prevHook up to date as we move along the list. The Hook obtained is returned.

Using a Hook

Now that we have made the Hook persistent to all updates, we can put it to work in a function component, similar to the _getM or _getM2 functions we crafted in the previous chapter.

Let's create a _useHook function this time that accepts an initialState value:

```
function _useHook(initialState) {
  let Hook
  if (isFiberMounting) {
    Hook = mountHook()
    Hook.state = initialState
```

```
  } else {
    Hook = updateHook()
  }
  return Hook.state
}
```

Based on whether the component is under the mount or not via an `isFiberMounting` flag, the preceding `_useHook` function obtains a persistent Hook. If it's at the mount, *React* assigns `initialState` to the Hook. For any other update, the Hook does not get touched. For all cases, `state` under the Hook is returned.

You may wonder how *React* determines the `isFiberMounting` flag; since it's wired more deeply with the engine, we put this material in *Appendix B – Current and WorkInProgress Scenes* at the end of this chapter.

So far we have gone through how *React* implements the Hook under the engine. We just bit the hard part, now let us take a look how we can use it.

What is a Hook?

Now that we have revealed the stripped-down version of the *React* Hook infrastructure and crafted a function using it, let's give it a spin in a function component:

```
const Title = () => {
  const a = _useHook(0)
}
```

The preceding a variable is assigned a 0 number upon the mount, and then it serves as a state for the rest of the updates.

`_useHook` is technically a *React* hook function. Though it's not an officially supported one, and we crafted it here to demonstrate the infrastructure, it has everything about being a hook function. Let's take a close look at it.

> **Note**
> To distinguish the educational hook that we crafted from the officially supported hook, we prefixed the hook name with _, as in _useHook.

We'll further explain the nature of a hook being a function as well as its calling order in the following section.

A hook is a function

A hook is a function that takes input arguments and returns a value, and it carries a `use` name prefix by convention.

If we take `useHook` as a generic hook, the following are sample usages of hooks with different input arguments:

```
const Title = () => {
  const a = useHook()
  const b = useHook(1)
  const c = useHook(1, 2, "Hello")
  const d = useHook({ text: "Hello World"})
}
```

A hook takes zero or any number of input arguments. An input argument can be used for the initial condition, as the `initialState` parameter in `_useHook`. It's important to know that not all input arguments are used for initialization purposes because, as you can see in the implementation, input arguments such as `initialState` are sent to each update, but it's up to the update whether the input argument needs to be used.

As a function, a hook can return a value if needed. The returned value can be designed in any format:

```
const Title = () => {
  useHook(...)
  const i = useHook(...)
  const [j, k] = useHook(...)
  const { value } = useHook(...)
}
```

Not all hooks return a value. If a value is returned, it can be `null`, a number, a string, an array, an object, or any JavaScript expression.

Since one return value can become another's input argument, it's not uncommon to see a chain usage of hooks, such as the following.

```
const Title = ({ text }) => {
  const i = useHook(...)
  const j = useHook(i)
  const k = useHook(i, j, text)
}
```

In the previous code, i and j are returned from two hooks and then injected into another hook to come up with k through input arguments. Also, a text prop is sent to a hook as an input argument. Practically, a hook statement does not differ too much from a local assignment statement.

All in all, a hook technically is a function. Don't be intimidated by it just because it's a hook. Most of the things you know about functions apply to hooks. That being said, a hook is a special function, and it comes with one caveat to be aware of – its calling order.

A hook's calling order

By now, we know that a hook function can be used many times in a function component without causing conflicts because each state points to a separate memory space:

```
const Title = () => {
  const a = _useHook(0)
  const b = _useHook("Hello")
}
```

Remember when we were crafting our naive version of _getM2 to support multiple states, we had to use a key to distinguish the a variable from the b variable? Now, with the Hook infrastructure, we don't do that anymore. Have you wondered how it is possible without a state key?

At the mount, before a first hook function for a is used in the function component, there's no Hook created yet:

```
const a = _useHook(0)
```

After running the preceding statement, *React* creates one Hook and puts it under the fiber. Then, it sees another hook function for b:

```
const b = _useHook("Hello")
```

After seeing the preceding statement, *React* creates another Hook and puts it after the first Hook following the linked list. We are done with the first mount update.

Now it comes to the second update; when it sees the first hook function for a again, it looks into the linked Hooks under the fiber and grabs the first Hook. Similarly, when it sees the second hook function for b, it continues looking into the list and finds the second Hook following the first one.

Essentially, *React* does not use a key because the order of the list serves as a key and the key is called the calling order of the hooks. As long as the first hook for a calls first and the second hook for b calls second, the location of the states stored under the list is marked correctly. So we don't have to consciously keep track of the key because after we write all the hook statements, the calling order should already be determined.

This design without an explicit key provided by the developer is quite easy to use. Except there's one caveat; if we can avoid running into it, this design works like a charm practically.

So, here's the caveat. This calling order isn't fixed during the code compilation; instead, it's determined at the runtime. What's the difference? The difference is that the runtime thing can be changed. To give you an example, we can set up a case using an `if` statement.

Conditional hook issue

Let's say we have the following `Title` component with two usages of hooks:

```
const Title = ({ flag }) => {
  const a = flag ? _useHook('a') : ' '
  const b = _useHook('b')
  return <h1>Hello World+{a}{b}</h1>
}
```

In the preceding code logic, what we intend to do is store the `'a'` and `'b'` chars in the a and b variables, respectively. Except, when the flag is `false`, an empty char `' '` is stored in the a variable.

To confirm whether the code works, let's make two updates to this component while flipping the `flag` prop. Suppose for the first update that the `flag` prop is set as `true` and for the second update, it gets changed to `false`. For this setup, it generates the following timeline sketch:

```
|T-------F---------------> flag
|a-------  ---------------> a
|b-------a---------------> b
```

At the first update, both a and b variables were assigned correctly. But when it came to the second update, the b variable was set to the `'a'` char. This is a bit weird since we never asked to set the `'a'` char to the b variable in the code. How could that happen?!

How could a _useHook('b') statement end up returning an 'a' char, and where does the 'a' char even come from? To answer the questions, we need to dig down into the Hooks under the fiber behind the Title component:

```
|T-------F----------------> flag
|a-------a----------------> Hook1
|b-------b----------------> Hook2
```

In the preceding timeline sketch, we printed out the states stored under two Hooks. Hook1 stored the 'a' char and Hook2 stored the 'b' char for both updates. Let's take a close look at the second update; what the compiler sees is the following code:

```
const Title = () => {
  const a = ' '
  const b = _useHook('b')
  return <h1>Hello World+{a}{b}</h1>
}
```

In the preceding arrangement of the code, we hardcode the flag prop with false. Because of that, the first usage of a hook for a is omitted, and we end up with one hook statement for b only. You can see this information in *Figure 3.3*, where we have both Hooks and what each hook statement reads:

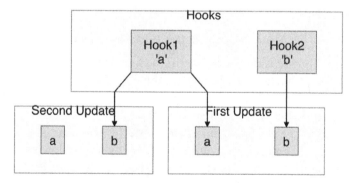

Figure 3.3 – Conditional Hook mismatch I

In the first update, the a and b variables read from Hook1 and Hook2. But in the second update, due to the first hook statement going, the b variable shifts and reads from Hook1. In this update, nothing reads from Hook2 either. Therefore, the b variable reads the 'a' char now.

> **Playground – Conditional hook I**
>
> Feel free to play with this online example at https://codepen.io/windmaomao/pen/RwLrxbp.

In this case, we changed the flag prop from T to F; we can also test this conditional case by changing the flag prop from F to T. Let's look at the timeline sketch if we do that:

```
|F-------T----------------> flag
|  -------b----------------> a
|b-------b----------------> b
|b-------b----------------> Hook1
|~-------b----------------> Hook2
```

From the preceding run, we printed out the a and b variables as well as two Hooks states. You can see that the a variables read the 'b' char in the second update! We can make the case clearer using *Figure 3.4*:

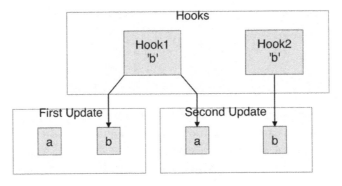

Figure 3.4 – Conditional Hook mismatch II

What happened to this case is the following. In the first update, we had one hook usage for b since the flag is F. Since this is the mount, the 'b' char was initialized to Hook1, and Hook2 was omitted. When it came to the second update, since Hook1 had been initialized already, the value can't be initialized again, thus it continued to hold the 'b' char. And Hook2 this time got finally initialized with the 'b' char. This is why both a and b stored the 'b' char after the second update. Pretty mind-blowing, isn't it? In a way, this case is worse than the previous one, of course; both are incorrectly implemented.

From these two cases, we can conclude that using the if statement with the hook statement leads to strange behavior. And this is all because the calling order of hooks gets changed from update to update, hence the state keys get messed up and the states can't be read as intended.

Playground – Conditional hook II

Feel free to play with this online example at https://codepen.io/
windmaomao/pen/oNGbEzq.

In fact, it's not only `if`; any hook statement involving a condition cannot be used. Here's another example:

```
const Title = ({ arr }) => {
  const names = arr.map(v => _useHook(v))
  return <div>{names.join('')}</div>
}
```

In the preceding code, we embedded a hook inside a loop iterating an `arr` array. Guess how many hook statements we would run into for this case? Not sure? Yes, you guessed right – we don't know how many elements the `arr` prop contains; it can only be determined at runtime. We will not walk through this case in detail, but you can see the code can easily run into a strange issue if the length of `arr` changes from 0 to 1, or 1 to 2, and so on.

React gives their recommendation in their documentation online: *"Don't call hooks inside loops, conditions, or nested functions. Instead, always use hooks at the top level of your React function, before any early returns."* Now you have a deeper understanding of why they said that.

React is fully aware of the severity of this issue because it could jeopardize the usage of a hook. Therefore, at the code compilation, the compiler actually alerts the developer when it spots the usage of conditional hook usage. Moreover, if it ever misses catching the case, at runtime, *React* monitors the hook list to find out whether there's any messing up of hook orders upon a new update. If it finds one, you see a warning, as shown in *Figure 3.5*:

```
▶Warning: React has detected a change in the order of Hooks
This will lead to bugs and errors if not fixed. For more inf
oks

    Previous render          Next render
    ------------------------------------------
1.  useContext               useContext
2.  useContext               useContext
3.  useReducer               useReducer
```

Figure 3.5 – React runtime warning for a conditional hook

Avoiding conditional hooks

So now we know we shouldn't have written any conditional hook statements, but how can we avoid it? Or, put another way, if we must implement some conditional logic involving hooks, what's the right way to do it?

The solution to this problem isn't difficult. We can still write conditional statements, just not conditional hook statements. As long as we have a fixed number of hooks and a consistent calling order, we can write the hook statement however we want.

Let's try to fix our examples, starting with setting flag from T to F first. Instead of declaring _useHook conditionally, we can declare two of them beforehand:

```
const Title = ({ flag }) => {
  const _a = _useHook('a')
  const b = _useHook('b')
  const a = flag ? _a : ' '
  return <h1>Hello World+{a}{b}</h1>
}
```

In the preceding code, we use an auxiliary _a variable to hold an 'a' char. The b variable holds a 'b' char as before. This way, no matter what, both hooks are maintained with a fixed calling order in all updates.

Now, with that, we can relocate the conditional logic part for a after the hook statements. We can verify whether this works by looking at the generated timeline sketch:

```
|T-------F--------------> flag
|a-------a--------------> Hook1
|b-------b--------------> Hook2
|a------- --------------> a
|b-------b--------------> b
```

Similarly, we can generate the timeline for changing flag from F to T:

```
|F-------T--------------> flag
|a-------a--------------> Hook1
|b-------b--------------> Hook2
| -------a--------------> a
|b-------b--------------> b
```

Both cases turn out to be correctly implemented now. The a variable can hold the 'a' char or an empty ' ' based on flag, and the b variable holds the 'b' char always.

> **Playground – Conditional hook I**
>
> Feel free to play with this online example at https://codepen.io/windmaomao/pen/KKXVQWV.

> **Playground – Conditional hook II**
>
> Feel free to play with this online example at https://codepen.io/windmaomao/pen/MWEKQQJ.

This writing of moving hook statements to the front of the function is recommended by *React*, and it can be applied to the loop case as well:

```
const Title = ({ arr }) => {
  const t = _useHook(arr)
  const names = t.map((v, i) => t[i] || '')
  return <div>{names.join('')}</div>
}
```

In the preceding code, we don't know the length of arr, so it's better not to loop through each hook statement inside the loop. Instead, we can store the entire arr to a state and then iterate this array afterward. This way, we eliminate the possibility of having a variable number of hook statements.

Luckily, the previously mentioned caveat is the only issue *React* hooks have, and if we run into a conditional statement, we can apply the "right" way by putting the hook statement on the front of the function.

In short, a *React* hook is a special function that allows persistent states for a function component. Out of the box, *React* provides quite a few hooks based on this infrastructure. Starting in the next chapter, we will get to know some of the common ones in detail, including useState, useEffect, useMemo, useContext, and useRef. And in *Chapter 9*, *Use Custom Hooks to Reuse Logic*, we will get toknow how to create our own custom hooks to meet our specific needs.

Summary

In this chapter, you have learned what makes a good state solution, and got to know how *React* builds the Hook to provide this solution. You also learned what a hook is and its calling order, as well as how to avoid running into a conditional hook issuein real applications.

In the next chapter, we will get into our first hook in the *React* family, with which *React* allows us to define a state to drive a UI display.

Questions and answers

Here are some questions and answers to refresh your knowledge:

1. What is a *React* hook?

    A *React* hook is a special function that allows us to have persistent states for a function component. The calling order of hooks is used as an internal key of the states, thus, when we use hooks, we don't need to specify a key. We can have as many hooks as we want under one function component, and each hook can be used for a different purpose.

2. How can we avoid conditional hooks?

    Each hook with a specific calling order gets stored under the hook list. *React* doesn't allow the change of this calling order at runtime, thus we should avoid it when using hooks inside a condition, a loop, or any structure that varies its calling order. Instead, we can move all hook statements to the front section of the function to pre-bake their calling orders while leaving the conditional logic afterward before the return statement.

Appendix

Appendix A – React Fiber

During the user session with a website, a series of actions is generated. We'd expect to have these actions dispatched and have changes applied back to the **Document Object Model (DOM)**. This cycle is what makes it a typical web experience.

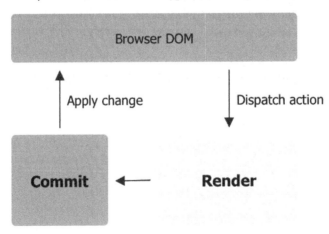

Figure 3.6 – React Fiber with Render and Commit phrases

What *React* does for us is to allow the dispatched action to update the changes to be reflected on the screen. *React* splits each update into two major phrases, the **Render** and the **Commit**, illustrated in the preceding figure. What a render does is go through all elements one by one and collect all the changes, whereas a commit applies the changes to the UI in one shot.

This engine has a codename, *Fiber*. To facilitate all this, *React* creates an internal object called a fiber to represent each element. As we have introduced, the element can be a classical element, such as a DOM element, or an artificial one, such as a function component. The benefits of having a layer between the physical DOM and *React* element are twofold.

A function component (or a class component) is easier for developers to organize their UI as well as their logic into a functional unit. Having a fiber wrapping a unit like that can offer some generic element behavior as well as add special handling to a specific element. For instance, we have introduced `updateFunctionComponent` for updating a function component, but for other elements, there are different update functions.

On the other hand, adding an extra layer to the UI engine allows optimization. In fact, React Fiber does not update to the screen blindly. In the first update, as in the mount, each fiber is created and all DOM elements get created from scratch. This update should be very close to the classical update.

However, everything else differs afterward. For a new update, the assumption is that only a small part of the screen needs adjusting. So, before *React* updates the screen, it goes through all fibers stored in the previous update and compares them with the new rendered elements. This comparison is referred to as reconciliation, which is to compare the new elements with previous DOM elements to come up with the new DOM changes that need to be applied in this update. *React* makes this reconciliation very efficient so that only necessary changes are applied to the screen.

The optimization is not only limited to reconciliation. To make sure things can be done efficiently, a fiber also serves as a unit of work. During each update, all fibers are sent to a pipeline where each fiber gets worked on one by one. There are certain advantages of doing that. The update work thus isn't treated as one or nothing anymore. The engine can finish 9 out of 10 units without hurting the integrity of the update job because it can now pause when it's out of resources and come back to finish the last unit once it gets enough computational time. One of the direct benefits is gaining a quick response to more urgent work in the browser.

Appendix B – Current and WorkInProgress Scenes

When we said that *React* internally creates a fiber for each element, we lied. Actually, for each element, *React* creates two fibers, and the name for these two fibers are `current` and `workInProgress`.

Imagine the user screen is like a stage with a curtain. The stage facing the audience is a current scene, while there's another work-in-progress scene behind the curtain where it can prepare what's next to show to the audience. While the audience enjoys watching the current scene, the work-in-progress scene is getting prepared at the same time. Only when the time is right is there a wheeler that rotates the current scene behind and pushes the work-in-progress scene to face the audience, as shown in *Figure 3.7*:

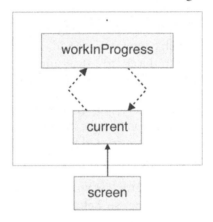

Figure 3.7 – React two scenes with current and workInProgress

This is a well-known mechanism behind any show business, including a computer screen. *React* is no exception. In order to facilitate the smoothness of a screen transition before/after the commit, it uses two scenes in memory, named `current` and `workInProgress`.

Initially, both scenes are empty, since the show hasn't started yet. We work on the `workInProgress` scene while `current` is empty; this step is called the **Mount**. It means every component needs to be created from scratch, thus the mount is relatively heavy. Once the preparation of `workInProgress` is done, the stage rotates so that `workInProgress` becomes `current`. In programming, it's just a pointer assignment.

Upon any future action, the `workInProgress` scene starts to be prepared again. This time, `workInProgress` doesn't need to be created from scratch since it can clone unchanged things from `current`, and this step is called the **Update**. Relatively speaking, the update can be a lot less demanding than the mount in terms of DOM access. Once the preparation of `workInProgress` is done, the stage rotates so that `workInProgress` becomes the new `current` scene.

During either the mount or the update, we pick `workInProgress` to work for the future scene while leaving `current` as the finished work from last time, except that during the mount, there's nothing in `current`. So, to tell whether any component is under the mount or the update, we can check whether `current` is empty:

```
const isFiberMounting = current === null
```

Unless you work on the engine, you wouldn't be given two scenes at the same time since the developer outside of the core works on `workInProgress` while the user watches `current`. To all of them, there's only one scene.

4

Use State to Jumpstart Components

In the previous chapter, we learned how *React* designs a *hook* infrastructure to provide the persistency of a function component. In this chapter, we will begin learning about the built-in hooks in *React*, starting with the useState hook. We will first explain how the concept of *state* is used in *React*, and then we will walk through the data structure and source code behind useState and describe some common use cases for changing states. We'll give useState a test drive, and at the end of the chapter, we'll provide two practical examples of applying useState to the Avatar and Tooltip components.

We will cover the following topics in this chapter:

- State in React
- useState design
- Dispatching states
- Test driving the useState hook
- useState examples

- Questions and answers
- Appendix

State in React

By now, you should have some idea of what a *state* is. To recap, a state is a piece of *memory* stored inside a fiber, introduced in *Chapter 3, Hooking into React*. When combined with *props*, a state can represent a *UI* screen deterministically.

Figure 4.1 – A fiber tree with a source fiber

For example, let's say we build a site and end up with a fiber tree (such as the one seen in *Figure 4.1*). When a user makes an action (such as a click), the action sends a signal via an event handler to a fiber (the red dot in *Figure 4.1*). We call this fiber a *source fiber*.

Now, say the dispatched event changes a counter from 0 to 1. *React* should schedule an update based on this user action and then prepare all of the **Document Object Model** (**DOM**) elements for the screen. Assuming the red lines are the fibers that need to be changed, how does React figure this out?

Upon receiving this update request, *React* goes through the fiber tree from the root. Quite a few fibers (shown as the gray lines) do not have anything to do with this update, so they are cloned from the previous scene. When the update arrives at the source fiber, let's imagine the fiber carries a function component and invokes an update function called updateFunctionComponent:

```
let updatingFiber = ...
function updateFunctionComponent(Component, props) {
  let prevHook = null
  let children = Component(props)
  ...
  reconcileChildren(children)
  return updatingFiber.child
}
```

We introduced the first part of the updateFunctionComponent function in *Chapter 3, Hooking into React*. The second part of this function takes the children that the Component function returns and converts them into fibers via reconcileChildren. At the end of the process, the first child fiber tells the engine what to work on next. This continues until all of the fibers under the source fiber are visited – that is, the red areas shown in *Figure 4.1*.

In this way, a state change propagates into the children fibers through that branch. When a parent gets updated, a child gets a new set of props before updating, thereby carrying the impact of the state. This is essentially how a state plays in the *React* ecosystem. Now, let's dive in and see how *React* creates the useState hook to support this behavior.

useState design

React provides a useState hook to manage the state within function components. The following code example shows its common usage:

```
const Title = () => {
  const [state, dispatch] = useState(initialState)
  const onClick = () => {
    dispatch(newState)
  }
  return <button onClick={onClick} />
}
```

The useState function takes an initialState argument as the input argument and returns a state object and a dispatch function. The dispatch function can be used to request a state change into a newState *object*.

Have you ever wondered how *React* designs the useState hook behind the scenes? Why does it return an array? How do we know if a new dispatch is successful or not? Most importantly, how can we be sure about the current state in each render?

To answer these questions, we will open up the engine and take a look inside. We will read through a stripped-down version of the source code to gain a bird's-eye view of the architecture relating to this hook before we get into its various uses. Let's start with the data structure first.

useState data structure

The data structure to make useState work includes a Hook type, a Queue type as well as an Update type, as shown in *Figure 4.2*:

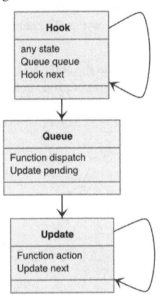

Figure 4.2 – The data structure of the useState hook

A Hook uses a state property to store the state as well as a next property that points to the next hook. We have already explained this architecture in *Chapter 3, Hooking into React*. What's new now is that in order to support the dispatch functionality, a queue property is added, where it provides a dispatch function to dispatch an action object with a new state. Within the queue, a list of updates is stored under a property called pending. The job of the queue is to maintain a list of pending updates to this fiber – this way, a user can dispatch multiple updates to the fiber.

An update is defined to hold an action function that needs to be provided by the user to calculate the next state. Each update is linked to another update via a property called next to form a circular linked list (see *Figure 4.3)*. The linked list is similar to how hooks are linked, except updates are linked in a circle, where the last update always points to the first update.

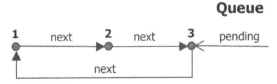

Figure 4.3 – A hook's queue with its pending updates

In the preceding figure, there are three updates in the queue with `pending property` points to the last one making `pending.next` point to the first update of the list. This circular list becomes handy when we need to insert or remove updates at the head or tail of the list.

Now that we have seen the data structure of `useState`, it's time for us to go over the source code and see how this data structure is utilized in the implementation.

The source code of `useState` is structured in a typical *hook* way in that it takes a path of either `mountState` or `updateState`, depending on if the fiber is under `mount` or `update` (as explained in *Chapter 3, Hooking into React*):

```
function useState(initialState) {
  if (isFiberMounting) {
    return mountState(initialState)
  }
  else {
    return updateState(initialState)
  }
}
```

Mounting a state

When a component is under `mount`, the `mountState` gets a hook by creating one:

```
function mountState(initialState) {
    const hook = mountHook()
    if (typeof initialState === 'function') {
      initialState = intialState()
    }
    hook.state = initialState
    hook.queue = {
      pending: null
      dispatch: dispatchAction.bind(
        null,
        updatingFiber,
        hook.queue
      )
    }
    return [hook.state, hook.queue.dispatch]
}
```

Then, it starts to perform the initialization work of the hook. Depending on the form in which the initialState object is provided, it can initialize the hook's state object with a value or a function:

```
useState(1)         // a value
useState(() => 1)   // a function
```

After initializing the state, it creates an empty queue object with no pending update. Moreover, it sets up a dispatch function and stores it under the queue object. Let's have a close look at this function, as it's one of the crucial parts of the useState hook.

Dispatching an action

The dispatch function is designed to dispatch an action with a new state. It's created with the help of a utility function, dispatchAction, which takes a fiber, a queue, and an action.

Upon assigning the dispatchAction function to the queue, it binds the updating fiber and the queue so that the dispatch function can accept the action object as the only input argument:

```
function dispatchAction(fiber, queue, action) {
  const update = {
    action
    next: null
  }

  const pending = queue.pending
  if (pending === null) {
    update.next = update
  }
  else {
    update.next = pending.next
    pending.next = update
  }
  queue.pending = update

  // Appendix A: Skip dispatch

  scheduleUpdateOnFiber(fiber)
}
```

The function takes an `action` object from its input argument then creates a new `update` object and appends this to the `queue` object. The preceding code relating to `pending` are all list operations, all of which append the `update` object to the end of the list while making sure the queue continues to form a circular linked list, as illustrated in *Figure 4.3*.

An `action` object can be in the form of a value or a functional updater, exactly as the `initialState` object is, thereby supporting both formats when we invoke the `dispatch` object. This is shown in the following example:

```
dispatch(1)          // a value
dispatch(() => 1)    // a function
```

After the queue is updated, it requests an update through a `scheduleUpdateOnFiber` function that essentially kicks *React* into the update process we introduced at the beginning of this chapter. This is the main pathway for how *React* handles a user action.

React comes with lots of optimizations inside the engine. Some of these are not publicly accessible because they are part of the engine code. For example, there is a hidden pathway where the dispatch or the entire update can be canceled without invoking the `scheduleUpdateOnFiber` function. If you are interested, you can find out more about this pathway in the *Appendix A – Skipping the dispatch* section at the end of this chapter.

Updating a state

After the component is mounted, the next time it gets updated and reaches to the `useState` hook, it goes into `updateState` and gets a hook by cloning one:

```
function updateState(initialState) {
    const hook = updateHook()
    const queue = hook.queue

    let updates = queue.pending
    queue.pending = null

    if (updates != null) {
        const first = updates.next
        let newState = hook.state

        let update = first
        do {
            const action = update.action
            newState = typeof action === 'function'
                ? action(newState) : action
            update = update.next
        }
    }
```

```
        while (update !== null && update !== first)
        if (!Object.is(newState, hook.state)) { … }
        hook.state = newState
    }
    return [hook.state, hook.queue.dispatch]
}
```

Once we have the hook, we can check if it gets any pending updates under the `queue.` `pending` object. The reason the `pending` object can have any update is that the `dispatch` function has been previously invoked. It goes through the first `pending.` `next` updates and iterates through them following the `update.next` update. For each update, it takes the stored `action` object and applies it to the previous stored state to form a `newState` object that gets stored back to the hook in the end.

The updated `newState` object gets compared to the previous `state` object to determine if it changes:

```
        // Appendix B - Bailing out an update
        if (!Object.is(newState, hook.state)) {
          didReceiveUpdate = true
        }
```

If it turns out the `newState` object differs from the previous state, *React* sets a `didReceiveUpdate` flag, indicating whether the updating fiber contains any change. The reason why *React* uses a global flag here is that there can be lots of other hooks attached to this fiber, therefore, it has to wait until all of the hooks are processed before it can determine if the fiber should be updated or bailed out. If you are interested in the details of the bailing out process, please refer to the pathway in the *Appendix B – Bailing out an update* section at the end of this chapter.

Returning the hook

For either the `mountState` or `updateState` function, the `state` and the `dispatch` function are returned:

```
    return [hook.state, hook.queue.dispatch]
```

They are returned in an array with two elements. The array format used here is interesting, as we could have used another format, such as an object with keys:

```
    return {
      state: hook.state,
      dispatch: hook.queue.dispatch
    }
```

The preceding key-value design would have worked as well. Instead, *React* decides to use an array due to one advantage that this has – that is, we don't have to remember the key name when referencing any of the values. Here are some examples demonstrating this:

```
const [state, dispatch] = useState("")
const [count, setCount] = useState(0)
const [a, d] = useState(null)
```

As you can see, we can rename the `state` and the `dispatch` functions using any name we want, as long as it fits logically at that moment. This becomes pretty handy practically.

All in all, the `state` and `dispatch` functions are directly mapped to the `state` object and the `queue.dispatch` function from the underlying hook. If the state has not changed, it gets the previous state returned. The `dispatch` function is created during the mount and keeps the same function instance for all future updates.

A walkthrough of useState

We have just gone through all of the `useState` hook's code. Just to make you feel better, *React* contains five times the amount of code that we just showed. With the stripped-down version, it's easy to understand the key workflow as it relates to the problem it's designed to solve and what approach it takes. Let's take a look at the workflow sketch in *Figure 4.4*.

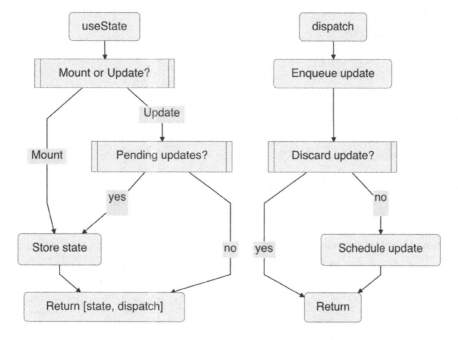

Figure 4.4 – The useState hook workflow

Let's explain what we are seeing in *Figure 4.4*. In an update, as a useState hook is invoked, it first checks if it's under mount or update. If it's under the mount, it stores the initialState, creates a dispatch function, and then returns. If under the update, it checks for any pending updates and applies them to a new state. In both cases, [state, dispatch] is returned.

When a dispatch function is invoked, it creates an update with the provided action object and appends it to the pending updates. Then, a request for a new update is scheduled to *React*.

It's important to note that the new update is the place where a state object is assigned. The purpose of the dispatch function is only to request a change, but *the real change does not apply until the next update*.

Now that we have gone through the design behind useState, we can talk about how to dispatch states in general in the next section.

Dispatching states

In this chapter, we have learned that the dispatch function, provided by the useState hook, allows us to request a change of state any time we want to. The input argument that represents an action can be a string, a number, an object, an array, or any *JavaScript* expression:

```
dispatch(state)
dispatch({ state })
dispatch([ state ])
dispatch(null)
```

We know that, internally, the input argument supports a functional update format as well:

```
dispatch(state => state + 1)
```

The benefit of using a functional update format here is that it has an opportunity to read the previous state before making a move toward the next state. This sometimes becomes useful if you build a new state that requires an old state.

A dispatched state is compared with the current state before making a final call if it changes. This means that not all dispatches end up with a state change. Take the following code as an example:

```
const [state, dispatch] = useState(1)
const onClick = () => { dispatch(3) }
```

If the state starts with its number as 1, we can change the state to 3 with the first click. For later clicks, it can't change the number to 3 because it's already 3. Therefore, upon multiple clicks, the changes taken are 1, 3, instead of 1, 3, 3, ... – no matter how many times the user clicks. Let's take a look at how this comparison is performed in detail.

Comparing states

We mentioned earlier that *React* uses the Object.is function whenever it compares two states. This is a *JavaScript* native function, which is quite similar to the *JavaScript* strict equality operator (===) and is used to determine whether two values are the same value.

For a primitive type, such as a number or a string, this comparison is straightforward:

```
1 === 1                   true
"Hello" === "World"       false
false === true            false
```

It's not difficult to understand that comparing the numbers 1 and 1 should return true and comparing the two strings Hello and World should return false.

JavaScript comes with seven primitive data types: string, number, bigint, Boolean, undefined, symbol, and null. These data types *cannot* be altered once they are created in memory:

```
null === null             true
undefined === undefined true
```

A *primitive comparison* is something we commonly understand as a *comparison by value*.

For a non-primitive type in *JavaScript*, such as an object or an array, a reference (also known as a pointer) is used to point to a particular memory space:

```
{} === {}                 false
v === v                   true
```

This means that if you allocate two new objects, they can't point to the same memory space. Therefore, comparing the two objects { } and { } should return false, even if both contain exactly the same *content*. In contrast, comparing the same object (for example, v and v) should return true, no matter how the content of the object changes. Let's take a look at an example to understand this better:

```
const [v, dispatch] = useState({})
const onClick = () => {
  v.abc = 3
  dispatch(v)
}
```

Can you guess if the previous dispatch does anything upon a user click? The answer is *no*. Changing an object's content doesn't qualify as a change from the `Object.is` function's point of view, as the v variable still points to the same memory location, even when one of its properties has changed.

The only way to cause a change in this case is to dispatch a state pointing to a different memory space, and we can do this by creating a new one:

```
const [v, dispatch] = useState({})
const onClick = () => {
  dispatch({ ...v, abc: 3 })
}
```

A new object is created with the help of JavaScript's **ES6** syntax ({ ...v }) by cloning the content of v while changing the abc property to 3. For readers who are interested in learning more about the *JavaScript ES6 syntax*, please refer to the *JavaScript ES6* section of *Chapter 10, Building a Website with React.*

It might take some time to get used to using the `Object.is` function or the strict equality operator (===). A simple question to ask yourself is this: *is the value to compare mutable?* If it is, it's compared by *reference*. If it's not, it's compared by *value*.

In React, if you can't manage a value change, you can't dispatch a change correctly. So, it's important to understand `object.is`, as it's used extensively for all hook value comparisons, as you'll see during the rest of this book.

Multiple dispatches

An interesting case arises when we perform multiple dispatches inside of one event handler. In *React,* multiple dispatches in a row are designed to be processed together, as in the following example:

```
const [state, dispatch] = useState(1)
const onClick = () => {
  dispatch(3)
  ...
  dispatch(5)
}
```

Upon the user clicking, if we invoke the dispatch (P-Code) function twice, it would only cause one change in the end because each dispatch appends an update to the queue. When we reach the next update, all registered actions in the queue are iterated to form a single new state. In our case, the state changes from 1 to 5, skipping 3. But why do two dispatches trigger only one update? Doesn't each dispatch invoke the `scheduleUpdateOnFiber` function?

Each dispatch does invoke `scheduleUpdateOnFiber` to kick *React* into the update process. However, this function is designed in such a way that it waits for all dispatches from the same action before making a final update. Therefore, with this functionality, multiple dispatches can be joined into one update operation as a deferred run.

A benefit of this is that you can write a `dispatch` statement as easily as an assignment statement without worrying that it might bring unnecessary work to the DOM. This is not only practically easy to use but also makes the update pretty performant.

Now that we have gone over the `dispatch` function, we can put the `useState` hook to use.

Test driving the useState hook

A state is one of the most common techniques in *React* for driving user interactions. Let's consider a component with a button. Each time we click the button, it increments a number and appends it to the `Hello World` string (see *Figure 4.5*).

Figure 4.5 – The Hello World counter

We can capture this *UI* behavior in a `Title` component:

```
const Title = () => {
  let [count, setCount] = useState(0)

  const onClick = () => {
    setCount(count + 1)
  }

  return (
    <>
      <button onClick={onClick}>+</button>
      <h1>Hello World+{count}</h1>
    </>
  )
}
```

Here, we use [count, setCount] to keep track of the count state. Then, we display count in the h1 element of the page and dispatch setCount in the click handler of the button element. Each time the button is clicked, it should increment the count value.

In order to confirm what happened under the hood, let's add console.log to two locations:

```
function Title() {
  let [count, setCount] = useState(0)

  const onClick = () => {
    setCount(count + 1)
    console.log('clicked', count)      ①
  }

  console.log('rendered', count)       ②
  return ...
}
```

The first one is placed after setCount to confirm what the count value is after each dispatch. The second one is placed before the return statement so that we can confirm when an update has arrived and what the count value is in that update. They are marked at ① and ②:

```
|-----0-----1-------2-----> clicked   ①
0-----1-----2-------3-----> updated   ②
```

From the updated series at ②, the number is incremented by 1 from the clicked series at ①. The count value started at 0 during the mount, and with each click, it quickly gets to a new update with an updated number, as shown in *Figure 4.6*.

The clicked series at ① confirms that the count value doesn't get updated to the new count + 1 value after the dispatch. Instead, it continues to hold the current state in the update where the onClick object is defined.

Figure 4.6 – The Hello World counter

Great! This is how we use useState in general. Let's take a look at another popular use of useState, which is to install it in a parent component and allow the child component to drive it.

Letting a child drive

It's very common to send a `dispatch` function from a parent component to a child component and expect the child to request the state change from the parent:

```
const App = () => {
  const [count, setCount] = useState(0)
  const onClick = () => {
    console.log('clicked', count)    ①
    setCount(count + 1)
  }
  console.log('rendered', count)    ②
  return <Title onClick={onClick} />
}
const Title = ({ onClick }) => {
  return <button onClick={onClick}>+</button>
}
```

In the preceding example, the `Title` component has a button, and when it is clicked, it changes the `count` state in the `App` component. We will set up two `console.log` statements to confirm the updates:

```
|-----0-----1------2-----> clicked    ①
0-----1-----2------3-----> updated    ②
```

It's working as expected – the clicks come from the child, but everything else is the same as the previous example. Basically, we have given the child the ability to change the `count` value created at the parent level.

This is actually quite handy. It tells us that no matter where we define the state, if its child (or grandchild) needs it, it can access it via a prop. This includes the state and the capability of changing the state. This is one of the most effective strategies for using state in *React* and we call it *lifting up*.

Lifting up to the parent

Due to its design, *React* doesn't allow information to be sent to an element directly. Instead, the required mechanism is to use a *prop* that passes the information from a parent to a child, then to a child's child, and so on.

In another way, to share information between two children, the information needs to be available to the parent first before sending it to each of the children:

```
const App = () => {
  return (
    <>
```

```
        <Title />
        <Content />
    </>
  )
}
const Title = () => {
  const [count, setCount] = useState(0)
  return <button>+</button>
}
const Content = () => {
  return ...
}
```

In the preceding setup, we have a parent, App, rendering two children, Title and Content. The count object installed in the Title object can't be accessed by either its sibling, Content, or its parent, App. So, to make the count object available to access, we need to relocate the count object to App:

```
const App = () => {
  const [count, setCount] = useState(0)
  const onClick = () => {
    setCount(count + 1)
  }
  return (
    <>
      <Title onClick={onClick} />
      <Content count={count} />
    </>
  )
}
```

In the preceding code, useState is declared in App, therefore, we can send the onClick object to Title, and we can send the count object to Content. Therefore, we can allow the sharing of things with a sibling by *lifting* those things to the parent. This highlights an important aspect of *React's* design: *if your parent has it, you can have it*. This is one of the most basic and effective behaviors we rely on when designing a *React* app.

> **Important Note**
>
> If you are a *React* beginner, you should try to work with props as often as you can. Not only are they easy to understand, but they're also a way to make sure everything is wired up correctly.

Now that we have had a test drive of the useState hook, let's look at two more practical examples of how real applications use useState to drive *UI* behavior.

useState examples

In this section, we are going to look at two examples of how the useState hook is applied in practice.

Making an avatar component

Let's say you want to display an image of a person that you have pulled from the internet. Most of the time, it will turn out to be a good picture (see *Figure 4.7*). But sometimes, an image can be unavailable to download due to network or permission issues. When this happens, the browser throws a broken icon (the logo in the middle of *Figure 4.7*), which is not as nice to look at. The latest UX research shows that if we replace any broken image icons with something more unique (such as a user's name or initials, as shown on the right of *Figure 4.7*), this improves the user experience.

Figure 4.7 – An avatar component using useState

In order to switch between an image and text, we can apply useState to define a condition. We will also need an event handler to notify us when an image URL is broken. If we put this logic together, we get an Avatar component:

```
const Avatar = ({ src, username }) => {
  const [error, setError] = useState(false)
  const onError = () => { setError(true) }
  return (
    <AvatarStyle>
      {error ? (
        <div>{username}</div>
      ) : (
        <img
          src={src}
          alt={username}
          onError={onError}
        />
      )}
```

```
      </AvatarStyle>
    )
  }
```

In the preceding code, first, we define a state, `error`, with `useState`. and then we set the initial state to `false`, assuming that there's no error before loading the image.

In the component's `return`, it follows this simple logic:

```
  { error ? A : B }
```

If `error` is `true`, it will display A. Otherwise, it will display B. In our case, A will return the user's initials and B will return an image. Therefore, it initially displays the image. If the image loads successfully, the job is done. However, if the image happens to fail, it fires an `onError` event handler. In the `onError` event handler, it makes a dispatch to flip the `error` flag to `true`. In the next update, as the `error` flag changes to `true`, it displays the user's initials. So, the job is done – sweet!

To make it easy to use, the `Avatar` component is built with two props, `src` and `username`, where the first prop is the image URL and the second prop is the username string. Here's what the code looks like:

```
const LOGO = 'https://gravatar.com/avatar/7aa1ac6'
const App = () => {
  return <Avatar src={LOGO} username="F" />
}
```

> **Playground – Avatar Component**
> Feel free to play with this example online at `https://codepen.io/windmaomao/pen/VwzaqEo`.

The `AvatarStyle` component is a style component that allows us to write CSS inside of a component. If you are interested in learning more about this approach, please refer to the *Adopting CSS-in-JS approach* section in *Chapter 10, Building a Website with React,* for more details.

Making a custom tooltip component

Here is another example of using `useState`. Say you have an avatar (you could borrow the one from the previous example), and when hovering over it, you'd like to see some tooltip text (as shown in *Figure 4.8*). This has to be a custom tooltip because we want it to allow a custom border, color, font, and even the inclusion of paragraphs. A browser's built-in tooltips won't provide these options in the `title` attribute.

Figure 4.8 – A custom tooltip component using useState

In order to support this pop-up effect, we can use `useState` to set up a Boolean state to indicate when the mouse hovers over the avatar area. We also need both event handlers to monitor when the mouse enters or leaves the avatar area. We can put this logic into a `Tooltip` component:

```
const Tooltip = ({ children, tooltip }) => {
  const [entered, setEntered] = useState(false)
  return (
    <TooltipStyle>
      <div
        onMouseEnter={() => { setEntered(true) }}
        onMouseLeave={() => { setEntered(false) }}
      >
        {children}
      </div>
      {entered && (
        <div className="__tooltip">
          {tooltip}
        </div>
      )}
    </TooltipStyle>
  )
}
```

We define a state, `entered`, and set its initial value to `false` (as when we first see this component, the tooltip will not be visible). We wire `setEntered` to the `onMouseEnter` and `onMouseLeave` event handlers to flip the state.

Notice that this time the `?` operator isn't used for the conditional display of the tooltip – instead, a `&&` operator is used:

```
{ entered && A }
```

That's because in `Tooltip`, there's no B. Depending on whether the mouse is in the right area or not, A is either displayed or hidden. Therefore, the `&&` operator is serving as a short circuit – if the condition isn't met, it skips the next statement.

The `Tooltip` component takes both `children` and `tooltip` as props, and this allows it to host any component as the `Avatar` object and any component as the tooltip content, as shown in the following code:

```
const TooltipBox = <div>Account</div>
const Title = () => {
  return (
    <Tooltip tooltip={<TooltipBox />}>
      <Avatar>
    </Tooltip>
  )
}
```

In the preceding code block, we define a custom `TooltipBox` component to pass in the `Tooltip` component via the `tooltip` prop.

Playground – Tooltip Component

Feel free to play with this example online at `https://codepen.io/ windmaomao/pen/qBXZvKV`.

This is the best part of the `Tooltip` component. It's not just designed as a component to suit the needs for one use case – instead, it's designed to be a mechanism that allows you to craft flexible tooltip behavior.

With `useState`, we can tailor our function components to be stateful engines, making it possible to handle a range of user interactions.

Summary

In this chapter, you learned what the concept of *state* is in *React*. You dug deeper into the `useState` design, which is divided into mounting a state and updating a state. We learned about various ways of dispatching states and ways to determine if a state has changed. Then, we also learned that a dispatch can support a value format or a functional updater format, and we learned that we can dispatch multiple times in one event handler. Then, we took `useState` for a test drive and learned how to send the state change to a child component via props. We also learned a common technique called *lifting up*, which involves lifting a state up to a parent. Last but not least, we designed two components – an avatar component and a tooltip component – to learn how to apply `useState` in the design of components.

In the next chapter, we will explore our second hook in the *React* family. We will also see how *React* defines an action called **effect** and allows you to invoke it after a state change.

Questions and answers

Here are some questions and answers to refresh your knowledge:

1. What is useState?

    The useState hook is a built-in hook in *React* that allows you to define a state within a functional component and dispatch an action to change it.

2. What is the most common use of useState?

    The useState hook is probably the most common hook in the *React* hook family. Whenever you need a variable to change *UI* elements, you can normally resort to useState to accomplish this. Touching a widget, clicking a vote-up button, hovering over an icon, toggling a checkbox, and much more can be implemented with the use of useState.

Appendix

Appendix A – Skipping the dispatch

We say that not all dispatched states end up with a change. But actually, not all dispatches end up with a successful dispatch. When a mouse clicks, it goes into the dispatch function. It has a special pathway, and when you hit that condition and find out there's no state change, it can return early without performing a dispatch:

```
function dispatchAction(fiber, queue, action) {
  ...

  if (NoWorkUnderFiber) {
    const currentState = queue.lastRenderedState
    const newState = typeof action === 'function'
      ? action(currentState) : action
    if (Object.is(newState, currentState)) {
      return
    }
  }
  scheduleUpdateOnFiber(fiber)
}
```

In the preceding dispatchAction function, a new state is computed when it detects there's no work currently under the fiber. The way it calculates the newState value is similar to how the calculation in the updateState function works, except it only deals with one action object here. Basically, it asks if the action causes a state change from the last updated state.

If it turns out that there's no change, it returns without an update, pretending nothing happened. This results in no *UI* updates whatsoever. This pathway is important because it can come very often (for instance, when the user keeps performing the same action over and over again without any state change).

Appendix B – Bailing out an update

For any fiber that has been updated, there is a collective flag that is added to it called didReceiveUpdate, which indicates if a change has taken place for the fiber. After the work starts on the fiber, any hook that causes a change can set this flag to true. Afterward, if the work is done and if the flag is still false, that means there's been absolutely no change for the fiber, so *React* bails out the fiber by cloning it from the previous scene and then moves on to the next fiber to work:

```
let updatingFiber = ...
function updateFunctionComponent(Component, props) {
  let prevHook = null
  let didReceiveUpdate = false
  let children = Component(props)
  if (!isFiberMounting && !didReceiveUpdate) {
    return bailout(updatingFiber)
  }
  ...
}
```

In the preceding updateFunctionComponent function, after the Component function is invoked, it checks two flags. One is isFiberMounting, as when the site is under mount, nothing can be bailed out since all of the fibers still need to be created. Another flag is didReceiveUpdate. When both are false, it kicks into the bailout of the fiber.

It bails out the fiber by cloning the children fibers from the current tree, which in turn carries all finished work over, including the old props and rendered *DOM*. Basically, by bailing out, it doesn't need to do the regular reconciliation work to figure out the new children fibers. And even better, if it turns out there's no work under the children of this fiber, the entire branch bails out. This corresponds to all the gray lines in *Figure 4.1*.

5

Use Effect to Handle Side Effects

In the previous chapter, we learned how `useState` is designed and how to use it to manage state changes in **React**. In this chapter, we will learn about using `useEffect` for managing *side effects*. We will first introduce what a *side effect* is, and then we will walk through the data structure and source code behind `useEffect` and provide various scenarios for invoking effects. We will also demonstrate a couple of pitfalls of using `useEffect` and discuss some ways to avoid them. At the end of this chapter, we'll use `useEffect` in two practical examples: *Finding the window size* and *Fetching an API resource*. The chapter also includes three bonus topics in the *Appendix* section: *React side effects, Flushing the passive effects,* and *Is a dispatch async*.

We will cover the following topics in this chapter:

- What is a side effect?
- Understanding `useEffect` design
- Creating effects
- Test driving `useEffect`
- `useEffect` examples

- Questions and answers
- Appendix

What is a side effect?

The following function has no side effect:

```
function add(a, b) {
  return a + b
}
```

This function is quite pure, in the sense that if it is invoked with the same set of input arguments, we should get the same result – that is, add(1, 1) will return 2. This type of *pure* function is easy to understand, test, and develop. The reason for this is that the function only depends on the input arguments and has no additional hidden dependency.

You might wonder what a hidden dependency could be? Believe it or not, it's quite easy to have one. In the following code, we'll intentionally introduce two lines and each will add a hidden dependency:

```
let c = 3

function add(a, b) {
  console.log(a, b)
  return a + b + c
}
```

The first line adds an external dependency from the c variable. Because c is a global variable, it bypasses the input argument list. If we invoke the add(1, 1) function now, it can return any number (or even a non-number). That's because c can be anything at the time when add is invoked. This applies to all *global* instances.

Let's take a look at another hidden dependency. Inside the add function, the first line adds an external dependency from the console.log function. Our intention here is to log the a and b variables to the screen. However, the console.log function could be anything at the runtime. For instance, if console doesn't exist, we could get an error when invoking console.log.

From these preceding examples, we can see that we could work with an *impure* function without knowing it. There's one important thing to bear in mind about impure functions – that is, they are prone to errors. For instance, in the preceding example, if someone changed any of the hidden dependencies, it would be difficult for the developer to know that. This can become a nightmare when it comes to refactoring the code.

To make our code robust, we tend to develop strategies to *avoid* hidden dependencies, either by removing them or containing their impact as much as possible so that we can be confident when developing and maintaining our code.

In general, there are two strategies to remedy impurity of functions. One way is to remove it by adding the dependencies to the input arguments so that they are not *hidden* anymore:

```
function add(a, b, c, log) {
  log(a, b)
  return a + b + c
}
```

This can be a very effective approach. With the preceding code change, the c variable and the log function are explicitly written as input arguments. It should take less effort to test this in the case of add(1, 1, 0, console.log). The only downside to this approach is that to implement it, you need to know the dependencies and declare them explicitly. This means the list of input arguments could get very long and impact the effectiveness of the function.

This brings us to the second strategy. Instead of removing the impurity, we can package and defer it to a later stage until we actually need to execute it. The following is an example of how we can *defer* an impurity:

```
function addFunc(c, log) {
  function add(a, b) {
    log(a, b)
    return a + b + c
  }
  return add
}
```

The addFunc function returns an add function. To use the add function,, we invoke addFunc to get a handle (also called a callback) of our add function back:

```
const add = addFunc(3, console.log)
```

So, what difference does this make? The dependency for c and log appears in the input arguments, so addFunc is a *pure* function. Essentially, we package any impurities and declare them one level up, so within the context of addFunc, the new add function looks and works a bit purer.

In a sense, we keep the original code, but we wrap it up to get a callback function so that we can execute it later. This helps protect the integrity of the main code while relocating the impurity. This deferred strategy is normally referred to as a *side effect*:

```
let c = 1, d = 2
function add() {
  c = 2
  const a = d
}
```

In the preceding code, the assignment of the c variable inside add is a side effect because it *changes* a global value; the assignment of the a variable is another side effect because it *reads from* a global value. From here, you can see that console is a solid side effect because it's an external service that writes to a terminal screen.

In a loosely connected open system, such as the web, a side effect is unavoidable. If you want to perform a range of actions and one action happens to not be defined by the internal system, then the action involves accessing an external system. Although we cannot avoid the side effect, we can package the side effect so that it accesses the external system at the right time.

Introducing passive effects

In React, a *side effect* refers to a case where we attempt to either *read from* or *write to* an *external system*. The external system can be a DOM element, an object such as a document or window object, or a fetch to a web server.

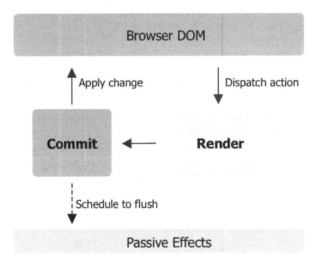

Figure 5.1 – React passive effects

Upon a user action, a *dispatch* is scheduled to trigger a *render* that is followed by a *commit* to form an update (as illustrated in *Figure 5.1*). During the update, React doesn't allow custom side effects to be invoked right away. Instead, React waits until the end of the commit before invoking them.

If there are two side effects encountered during the update, both are deferred and then invoked one by one after the *commit*. Effects such as these are referred to as the passive effects internally. Passive effects are one of several types of effects supported by React. If you are interested in the other types of effects, please refer to the *Appendix A – React side effects* section at the end of this chapter.

It is referred to as *passive* due to the way it's invoked during the update. React allows us to invoke a passive effect in each update or to conditionally invoke it when responding to a value change. Therefore, the effect isn't actively tied as in the case of a user event, but instead, upon a value change, the effect gets created, queued, and then invoked later. In a way, the effect can be invoked through a passive "event".

A passive effect is modeled as a callback function. In this instance, let's say it's called `create`. Invoking the `create` function executes the effect and returns a `destroy` function to perform the cleanup job associated with the effect.

Now that we know what a React effect is, let's dive in and see how a `useEffect` hook is designed to facilitate this process.

Understanding useEffect design

React provides a `useEffect` hook to set up a callback to be invoked after an update:

```
const Title = () => {
  useEffect(() => {
    window.title = "Hello World"
    return () => {
      window.title = "Notitle"
    }
  }, [])
}
```

The `useEffect` function takes a callback function called `create` as its first input argument to define the effect. In the preceding example, the effect sets the `window.title` to be `Hello World` when the component is mounted.

A `create` function can return a function called `destroy` to perform the cleanup. The interesting thing here is that the `destroy` function is provided by the `create` function as a return value. In the preceding example, the cleanup reverts the `window.title` object back to `NoTitle` when it is unmounted.

The second parameter in the `useEffect` argument list is a dependency array called `deps`. If `deps` is *not given*, the effect gets invoked each time during each update, whereas when `deps` *is given*, the effect only gets invoked upon a change from the `deps` array.

The useEffect hook's data structure

In this section, we are going to explain how `useEffect` is designed by taking a stripped-down version of the source code as an example. First, let's take a look at the data structure that makes it happen.

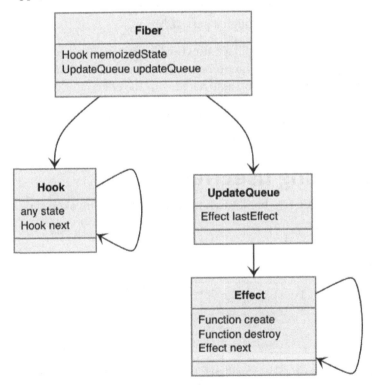

Figure 5.2 – The data structure for the `useEffect` hook

To keep track of effects, React creates an `updateQueue` property under a fiber of the `UpdateQueue` type (as illustrated in *Figure 5.2*). Inside this queue, a list of effects is stored under the `lastEffect` property. Effects are linked together using a circular linked list (see *Figure 5.3*), similar to the pending queue that we see in `useState`:

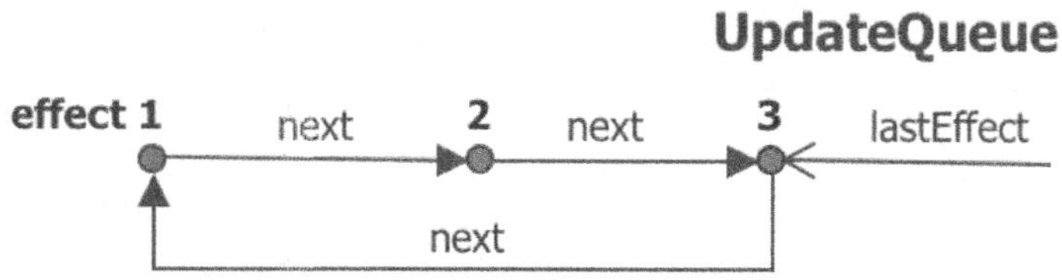

UpdateQueue

Figure 5.3 – A fiber's update queue for useEffect

Each effect in the list, it stores the effect function in the `create` property and the cleanup function in the `destroy` property.

The `useEffect` hook follows a typical hook setup where it takes the path of either `mountEffect` or `updateEffect`, depending on whether the fiber is under mount or update, via the `isFiberMounting` flag (as explained in *Chapter 3, Hooking into React*).

```
function useEffect(create, deps) {
  if (isFiberMounting) {
    mountEffect(create, deps)
  }
  else {
    updateEffect(create, deps)
  }
}
```

The `useEffect` hook takes the `create` function as well as the `deps` array and it does not return any value.

Mounting an effect

When the component is under mount, the `mountEffect` function first creates a hook:

```
function mountEffect(create, deps) {
  const hook = mountHook()
  hook.state = pushEffect(
    create,
    undefined,
    deps,
  )
}
```

Once it gets a hook, it stores the effect under the hook's `state`. The effect is created with the `pushEffect` function:

```
function pushEffect(create, destroy, deps) {
  const effect = {
    create,
    destroy,
    deps,
    next: null,
  }
  let queue = updatingFiber.updateQueue
  if (queue === null) {
    queue = { lastEffect: null }
    updatingFiber.updateQueue = queue
    queue.lastEffect = effect.next = effect
  }
  else { … }
    queue.lastEffect = effect
  }
  return effect
}
```

The `pushEffect` function creates an effect with all of the effect information, such as `create`, `destroy`, `deps`, and `next`. Then, it finds the `updateQueue` function under the currently updating fiber. If the queue is empty, the new effect gets attached. Otherwise, the new effect is appended to the queue. Either way, it appends the new effect as the `lastEffect` object in the queue. Since it's a circular linked list, after all of the previous pointer operations have taken place, it makes sure the `lastEffect.next` object still points to the first effect in the list.

Updating an effect

After the component is mounted, the next time it gets updated and reaches in the `useEffect` hook, it goes into `updateEffect` and gets the hook by cloning one:

```
function updateEffect(create, deps) {
  const hook = updateHook()
  let destroy = undefined

  const prevEffect = hook.state
  destroy = prevEffect.destroy
  if (deps) {
    const prevDeps = prevEffect.deps
    if (areDepsEqual(deps, prevDeps)) {
      return
```

```
      }
    }
  hook.state = pushEffect(
    create,
    destroy,
    deps,
  )
}
```

Once we have the hook, we can check the previous effect set in the mount and compare whether the deps array has changed. If the deps array hasn't changed from the prevDeps object stored in prevEffect, it returns without pushing the effect to updateQueue.

A utility function called areDepsEqual is used to compare the current and previous dependency arrays. We will examine this function in detail in the *Creating effects* section later in this chapter.

Scheduling effects

There's something very special about effects: effects are pushed into queue under each fiber, but they are scheduled around the time the screen is about to change.

For each effect, there are two callback functions that need to be scheduled: one is create and one is destroy. Taking create as an example, each create function is collected into a list via the enqueueEffect function:

```
function enqueueEffect(fiber, effect) {
  effectCreateList.push(effect)
  if (!rootDoesHaveEffects) {
    rootDoesHaveEffects = true
    scheduleCallback(() => { flushEffects() })
  }
}
```

The preceding enqueueEffect function takes the fiber and the effect and pushes it into the effectsCreateList array. It then schedules the flushEffects callback. The reason why the array doesn't get processed (or flushed out) the right away is that it has to wait until the end of the update. Here, React uses a global flag (rootDoesHaveEffects) to make sure it only triggers this schedule once.

The same process happens to each destroy function as well. For each update, we end up with two lists of effects: one for effectCreateList and one for effectDestroyList. Although similar, these two lists don't necessarily contain the same list of effects because some effects don't have the destroy callback. Moreover, when the component gets unmounted, the destroy callback needs to be added to effectDestroyList.

The scheduleCallback function is quite interesting. Instead of flushing and executing the effects right away, it does this a bit later, just like an asynchronous task in a new **JavaScript** task. If you are interested in the details of this, please refer to the *Appendix B – Flushing passive effects* section at the end of this chapter.

Flushing effects

It is only after the screen has been updated with the DOM changes that React can visit the effects lists again:

```
function flushEffects() {
  effectDestroyList.forEach(effect => {
    const destroy = effect.destroy
    effect.destroy = undefined
    if (typeof destroy === 'function') {
      destroy()
    }
  })
  ...
}
```

The preceding code goes over effectDestroyList, and each destroy function found, it gets invoked. After all of the destroy functions have been invoked, React flushes out the effects list for create:

```
function flushEffects() {
  ...
  effectCreateList.forEach(effect => {
    const create = effect.create
    effect.destroy = create()
  })
}
```

In the preceding code, effectCreateList gets flushed out by invoking the create function under each effect object. The result of the create function is then taken as the destroy function.

Notice the order in which React goes through both lists – it starts with destroy and then goes to create. Since both lists are collected from all of the fibers, there's a chance that the create function could contain a reference to a variable of a component that is going to be destroyed or cleaned up. In order to give the create function a chance to be fully aware of this situation, destroy functions need to be called before this happens. In short, all previous effects need to be cleaned up before new effects can be considered.

A walk-through of the useEffect hook

This is hard work, and we have just gone through a stripped-down version of the useEffect hook's source code. To help us understand this from a higher level, the following diagram outlines the useEffect hook in terms of the effects workflow in React (see *Figure 5.4*):

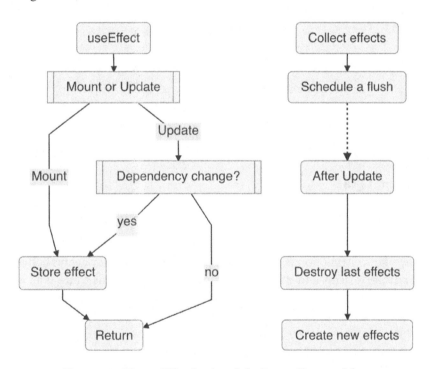

Figure 5.4 – The useEffect hook and the React effects workflow

Let's do a quick run-through of *Figure 5.4*. In an update, as a useEffect hook is invoked, if the component is under mount, it creates the effect. If the component is under update, it creates the effect depending on whether there are any dependency changes. If there's no change to the dependency array, the effect is skipped. In all cases when the effect is created, it gets appended to the fiber's updateQueue and stored under the hooks' state.

Right before the screen update, React takes all of the effects from all of the fibers and schedules a flush (denoted by the dotted line in *Figure 5.4*). After all of the fiber changes are applied to the DOM, React flushes them out by invoking them one by one, starting with the previous `destroy` effects and following them with the new `create` effects.

Creating effects

An effect can be skipped. As a matter of fact, an effect needs to be created in an update for it to take effect. This behavior is captured by a dependency array called `deps`. React uses a utility function called `areDepsEqual` to help decide whetherthis array changes. Let's take a closer look at this function:

```
function areDepsEqual(deps, prevDeps) {
  if (!prevDeps) {
    return false
  }

  for (let i = 0;
       i < prevDeps.length && i < nextDeps.length;
       i++)
  {
    if (Object.is(deps[i], prevDeps[i])) {
      continue
    }
    return false
  }
  return true
}
```

The `areDepsEqual` function is used to compare two dependency arrays between the previous `prevDeps` array and the current `deps` array and returns `true` if all of the elements match. Though this sounds easy to carry out, it can run into various scenarios depending on the elements of the dependency arrays. We'll explain all of the scenarios in the following list:

- **No dependency**:

  This is the default case for when `prevDeps` is not provided and the usage omits the array:

  ```
  useEffect(fn)
  ```

  When this happens, the `areDepsEqual` function always returns `false`, and so the effect gets created in each update.

- **Empty dependency**:

    When a dependency array is provided but with no elements in it – this means the effect doesn't depend on anything:

    ```
    useEffect(fn, [])
    ```

    In the case of an empty dependency, it makes areDepsEqual return true for all updates except the first one because, for the mount, the deps array still is considered to be changed from undefined. Therefore, the effect gets created once and after this, it does not get created anymore.

- **Some dependencies**:

    When the elements of deps are not empty, each element between the previous and current dependencies performs an Object.is comparison. We have already discussed the Object.is function in detail in *Chapter 4, Use State to Jumpstart Components*. Here, each element pair goes through this comparison to determine whether the array changes:

    ```
    useEffect(fn, [a, b])
    ```

    Other than the mount, if any of the elements change, such as a or b, the effect gets created.

Creating and destroying

If a destroy function is given from the effect create function, this case also needs to be taken into consideration. Remember, we have two separate arrays keeping track of both mounted and unmounted cases. In general, the destroy function is invoked before the create function is invoked.

So, here's a quick list to summarize all of these cases.

- It runs create once after the mount.
- For any deps changes, it runs destroy and create once.
- It runs destroy once after the unmount.
- If the destroy function is not provided, this process reduces to a single case below.
- It runs for any deps change, including the mount.

Now that we have gone through the useEffect hook's design as well as all of the scenarios of invoking the callback, let's take the useEffect hook for a test drive.

Test driving the useEffect hook

The effect callback is defined in the `useEffect` hook's first input argument:

```
function Title() {
  useEffect(() => {
    window.title = ""
  })
}
```

The most common way of using the `create` function can be defined by using the **JavaScript ES6** syntax with an inline function, `(() => {})`. For readers interested in learning more about *JavaScript ES6*, please see the Embracing *JavaScript ES6* section in *Chapter 10, Building a Website with React*.

One of the interesting facts about this effect function is that, thanks to JavaScript *closures*, it can access all of the variables defined in the functional component:

```
function Title({ text }) {
  const a = 2
  useEffect(() => {
    console.log(a)
    console.log(text)
  })
}
```

The `create` callback function in the preceding code references both the `a` variable and `text`. Without the JavaScript closure, both variables would have to be passed into the inline function through the input arguments explicitly.

Another interesting fact about the `useEffect` hook is that the effect is a callback where it's quite common to see an effect involving a state changed inside. Let's take a look at one example:

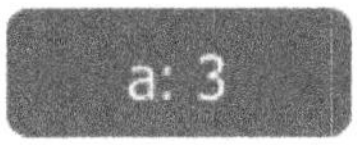

Figure 5.5 – A button with clickable text

Let's say we have a `Title` component that gets a `text` prop. Inside, it has a button. When this gets clicked, it can increment a `count` state. Initially, the `count` value is set to 0, and whenever the `text` prop changes, it can reset the `count` value back to 0. Notice that the user clicking and the `text` prop change could be entirely unrelated and driven by different mechanisms. The former comes from the user action, whereas the latter comes from the change from the parent components::

```
const Title = ({ text }) => {
  const [count, setCount] = useState(0)
    useEffect(() => {
    setCount(0)
  }, [text])

  const onClick = () => {
    setCount(count + 1)
  }

    console.log('count', count)
    return (
    <button onClick={onClick}>
      {text}: {count}
    </button>
  )
}
```

To implement the described behavior, we apply `useEffect` to dispatch `setCount` with the `deps` array set to the `text` prop. The following code example shows the timeline sketch for two clicks and one text change from the a letter to the b letter:

```
|-----x-----x------------> click
a----------------b------> text
R-----R-----R-----RR-----> update
0-----1-----2-----20-----> count
```

As the mount starts, the first update starts with the text as a and the count as 0. It also creates an effect, but since the `count` value is already 0, the `setCount` dispatch is skipped.

As the user makes the first click, the `onClick` event handler is invoked, therefore setting count to 1. The same applies to the second click in order to arrive at the `count` value of 2. When the parent component changes the `text` prop from a to b, it raises another update.

In the same update, the unchanged `count` value is printed out again. But this time, the dependency array of `useEffect` detects the change due to `[text]`. Therefore, it creates an effect to invoke `setCount(0)`. As we know that the `setCount` schedules another update, it will bring the `count` back to 0 afterward.

> **Playground – Button with parent text**
>
> Feel free to play with this example online at `https://codepen.io/windmaomao/pen/rNGOVor`.

Wow! This is how `useEffect` works. By using `setState` inside the callback, an additional update can be requested to update the screen. So, the effect takes effect in a different update. Also, to make the effect work, the `deps` array needs to be wired with the right state change because if we miss it, the effect can be stalled. Let's take a look at one example when this happens.

Missing dependencies

Let's go back to a simple setup:

```
const Title = () => {
  const [count, setCount] = useState(0)

  useEffect(() => {
    console.log(count)
  }, [])
}
```

If you intend to print out `count` every time it changes, the preceding code misses the right dependency – the correct one should be `[count]` instead of `[]`.

If this example is too obvious, let's try a less obvious one:

```
const Title = ({ text }) => {
  const [count, setCount] = useState(0)

  useEffect(() => {
    console.log(text + count)
  }, [text])
}
```

In the preceding code, we introduce a `text` prop and put it in the `deps` array. In this case, what we get is that when the `text` changes, it prints out `text` + `count`. However, if the `count` value changes due to a user's click, the screen wouldn't change. To fix this, we can add the `count` value to the dependency array:

```
useEffect(() => {
   console.log(text + count)
}, [count, text])
```

A pattern seems to emerge here – if an effect callback uses a variable, that variable needs to be in the `deps` array. This statement is practically 99.9% true. If you intentionally do not want to update the screen when a variable changes, you can skip adding it to the dependency array. However, this is not recommended by React. React even adds an **ESLint** plugin (`eslint-plugin-react-hooks`) to help us spot the cases where we have missed a potential dependency.

You might wonder why React doesn't want us to miss any dependencies. This is because in React, every value (or state) should be in-sync with the current screen and there can't be exceptions to this rule by default.. In *Chapter 8, Use Ref to Hide Stuff*, we will show you a recommended way if you insist on keeping things hidden from React.

Now that we have seen cases that have used both effects and states , let's take a look at another example of when we might run into problems with them.

Infinite loops

Combining *state* and *effects* can cause another interesting problem because an effect can change a state and therefore schedule a new update, and then the new update can create a new effect and change a state, and this can continue indefinitely. This could lead to an *infinite loop*.

We can demonstrate this with a quick example:

```
function Title() {
  const [count, setCount] = useState(0)
  useEffect(() => {
    setCount(count+1)
  }, [count])
  return <h1>{count}</h1>
}
```

In the preceding code, there's an effect that increments a `count` state after any `count` change. After invoking `setCount`, in the next update, `useEffect` would detect a change from the dependency array and thereby invoke `setCount` again. Because every time this happens we get a new `count` number, this process wouldn't stop, as you can see in the following timeline sketch:

```
RRRRRRRRRR> update
0123456789> count
```

Normally, we wouldn't do this intentionally, but we can accidentally run into exactly this scenario in a more complex setup, especially when many different states and effects are involved. It's our job to avoid an infinite loop whenever possible since this isn't accounted for by React.

So, how do we deal with an infinite loop in code? We can break out of a loop with an `if` statement, and this is normally the most cost-effective approach:

```
useEffect(() => {
  if (count >= 1) return
  setCount(count+1)
}, [count])
```

In the preceding code, after we add the `if` statement on the first line inside the effect, the timeline confirms that we don't have an infinite loop anymore:

```
RR--------> update
01--------> count
```

As you can see, it's not too difficult to break out of a loop. You can think of this as an equilibrium state that you want to reach – the effect does need to be triggered for a state change, but once an equilibrium state is reached, it stops without continuing the loop.

Now that we have gone over how `useEffect` is used, let's take a look at two practical cases for applying it.

useEffect examples

The `useEffect` hook is normally used for any side effect – whether that is to read from an external object or write to an external object. In the following sections, we are going to see two more examples: *Finding the window size* and *Fetching an API resource*.

Finding the window size

Let's say that we want to know the current browser window size at runtime so that a greeting title can fit perfectly onto the screen (see *Figure 5.6*):

Figure 5.6 – Finding the window size

This can be done normally with a **CSS** media query, but this time, we want to do it via *JavaScript*, as a runtime *JavaScript* variable obtained can be sent for purposes other than CSS usage:

```
const Greeting = () => {
  const [width, setWidth] = useState(0)

  useEffect(() => {
    function handleResize() {
      setWidth(window.innerWidth)
    }
    window.addEventListener("resize", handleResize)
    handleResize()

    return () => {
      window.removeEventListener("resize", handleResize)
    }
  }, [setWidth])
  const on = width > 600
  return <h1>{on ? "Hello World" : "Hello"}</h1>
}
```

The useEffect hook is a good fit here. After the component is mounted, we can listen for a resize event provided by the window object. Once it starts to listen to the event, every time the window resizes, it kicks off a handleResize function that sets the width state to the new window size. We also invoke handleResize at the mount to get the initial window size.

In this example, if the current width is greater than 600 px, we know that it can fit the Hello World string on screen. Otherwise, the Hello string will be used. This shows that we can control the display based on the window size on the fly with *JavaScript*.

> **Playground – Finding the Window Size**
>
> Feel free to play with this online example at `https://codepen.io/windmaomao/pen/BadRoNN`.

In order to prevent a memory leak, we return a `destroy` function from the `useEffect` callback where the registered event listener is removed when the component is unmounted.

There's a subtle detail to be aware of here – the dependency array has `setWidth` in it because we reference `setWidth` inside the `useEffect` function. If you remember from *Chapter 4, Use State to Jumpstart Components*, we know the `setWidth` function instance doesn't get changed after the mount, so actually, `[setWidth]` can be optional here. But React insists that we add this because when `setWidth` changes, the effect needs to be re-created.

Fetching an API resource

One popular use of `useEffect` is to fetch an API resource and display the data on screen:

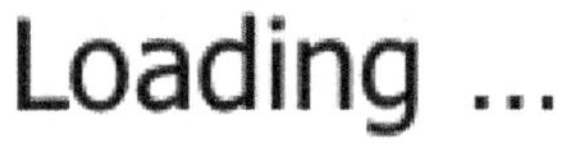

Loading ...

Figure 5.7 – Fetching an API resource, loading status

The idea here is to use the `fetch` JavaScript function to get the resource. During loading, the screen should say `loading...` (as in *Figure 5.7*). And after the resource is successfully fetched, the `loading...` string should be dismissed and replaced with the fetched text on the screen:

```
const Title = () => {
  const [text, setText] = useState("")
  const [loading, setLoading] = useState(true)

  useEffect(() => {
    fetch("https://google.com").then(res => {
      setText(res.title)
      setLoading(false)
    })
  }, [setText, setLoading])

  if (loading) return "loading..."
  return (<h1>{text}</h1>)
}
```

In the preceding code, we use a `text` state to store the fetched text and a state `loading` flag to store the loading status. A `useEffect` hook is used to fetch the resource and when it's successful, it updates the `text` and `loading` flag.

> **Playground – Fetching an API Resource**
>
> Feel free to play with this online example at `https://codepen.io/windmaomao/pen/ZEJKbev`.

In this case, the effect doesn't return anything. There's actually a cleanup to do in this case, but we will wait until *Chapter 8, Use Ref to Hide Stuff,* to explore that in detail.

Notice that an `if` statement is used before the `return` statement. In *Chapter 3, Hooking into React*, we mentioned that `if` cannot be used in between hook statements. So, in this case, we move it after all of the hook statements and put it right before the last return statement.

In this case, the `if` statement acts as a short-circuit. If the `loading` status is `true`, it does not go any further other than returning a `loading...` string. This `if` statement approach is one of the most cost-effective ways to make sure the screen only renders material when it's available.

Summary

We really did a lot in this chapter. First, we got to know what a side effect is, and we dug deeper into the `useEffect` hook's design. We discovered how an effect can be created and then later invoked after a UI update. We also learned about various scenarios for creating effects based on dependency arrays. After that, we walked through the pitfalls of using `useEffect` with missing dependencies, staled values, and infinite loops. Last but not least, we learned to apply `useEffect` in practical components, such as the examples of finding the window size in a browser and fetching API resources from an online server.

In the next chapter, we will discover our next hook in the React family and focus on how to apply an optimization to boost performance by using values from a previous update.

Questions and answers

Here are some questions and answers to refresh your knowledge:

1. What is a side effect?

    A side effect is when a function relies on or modifies something outside of its input arguments. A very common side effect is the use of `console.log` inside a function.

2. What is `useEffect`?

    The `useEffect` hook is a way of defining a side effect callback to be invoked after a screen update in React. The effect can be invoked every time or when one of its dependencies changes. Therefore, the `useEffect` hook can be also used for listening for value changes.

3. What are the most common uses of `useEffect`?

    The `useEffect` hook is a common hook in the React family. If used along with the `useState` hook, it can easily communicate with external resources and bring results on screen. External resources can be web servers, DOM elements, `window` objects, `document` objects, or any third-party entities.

Appendix

Appendix A – React side effects

When it comes to React, the most well-known effects are passive effects, as introduced and explained in detail in this chapter. However, React supports different kinds of effects, and in the future, it might add more. The two others currently are *mutation effects* and *layout effects*.

All effects are shared with certain features, such as getting collected from the fibers before the screen gets updated. But they also differ in some ways. Take the *mutation effects* as a first example. Under the engine, these kind of effects are the most important effects because each mutation effect tracks the addition, removal, or change of a DOM element. Therefore, all fiber reconciliation ends up with mutation effects that get committed to the screen. The mutation of the DOM elements is also part of the update, or more accurately, the *commit* phrase of the update. While the passive effects run after the update, all mutation effects happen before the passive effects.

To remedy the fact that passive effects run after the update (because by then it might be too late to perform a certain action), the *layout effect* is created to be invoked a bit earlier. Everything about the layout effect is similar to the passive effect, except it gets invoked right after the mutation effect and flushes out before the end of the update. The relationships and timing between all three kinds of effects can be summarized in the following commit stage outlined in *Figure 5.8*:

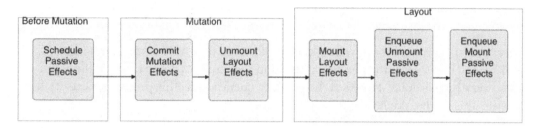

Figure 5.8 – React effects during the commit phase

Note that during the commit stage, only the mutation and layout effects get flushed out.. The passive effects get scheduled initially and later enqueued, but not flushed out until after the commit. Please read on to the *Appendix B – Flushing passive effects* section for more details.

Appendix B - Flushing passive effects

In order to understand how passive effects are scheduled and flushed, we need to first mention *JavaScript tasks*.

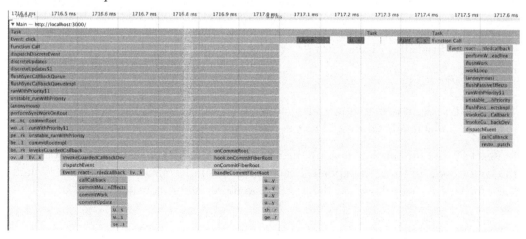

Figure 5.9 – JavaScript tasks

In *Figure 5.9*, we can see three *JavaScript* tasks. What is a task? A *task* is any *JavaScript* code that is scheduled to run by the standard mechanism. In the first task on the left, we finished one update. Normally, that's all we need to know about running *JavaScript* code.

However, because *JavaScript* is a single-thread engine, during the execution of the current task, there can be more work added to the pending queue. A typical example is a `setTimeout` call, which adds the callback to the queue instead of invoking it right away in the same task. API calls (like promises) normally fall into this category as well. This is the main reason why these callbacks are referred to as *asynchronous operations*.

There's no specification for how long each task should take. When one task finishes, it looks for all the work in the pending queue and then invokes it one task at a time, and after everything is done, it looks at the pending queue again. This process repeats itself forever. This is what the *JavaScript* engine does.

In our case, we have a very short-lived task (middle task in *Figure 5.9*) followed by a third task. Guess what – this is when the flushing out of passive effects begins. From this, we can be sure that the callback in the `useEffect` callback is invoked asynchronously.

We mentioned that the multiple state dispatches are also bundled and executed in a deferred way – so is a `setState` dispatch also an asynchronous call? To answer that question, please read on to the *Appendix C – Is a dispatch asynchronous?* section.

Appendix C – Is a dispatch asynchronous?

Since passive effects are invoked in a new task, at this point, you might wonder whether a `setState` dispatch is run in the same task or in a new task. This is a very good question.

To answer this, we need to have a reference point in time. Let's say we have an event handler, and inside it, we have a `setState` dispatch call:

```
onClick = () => { setState(1) }
```

The `onClick` event is an event that is requested as a callback via a user action. Let's say that the task that invokes the `onClick` event is called *Task 1*.

In React 17 (not the current version), the `setState` code is sync, which means it runs in the same *Task 1* for the entire update. React decides it's more efficient to finish them all in the same task. So, why do we say the `setState` object is normally deferred?

```
onClick = () => {
  setState(1)
  // state value isn't changed yet
}
```

That's because right after `setState`, the value hasn't been changed yet. Only the next update will set the state to the new version. But calling `setState` an async operation isn't exactly accurate (if not wrong) because all of this process is performed in the same *JavaScript* task.

What if we put `setState` in a `useEffect` hook? Does this passive effect change the sync or async discussion?

```
useEffect = (() => {
  setState(1)
}, [])
```

By now, we know that the `useEffect` callback gets invoked in a new *JavaScript* task – let's say this task is called *Task 1*. And the `setState` runs in the same *Task 1*. This makes it behave in quite a similar way to an event handler, such as in the case of `onClick` discussed previously. For this reason, we could also think of a passive effect as an *"event"* that is more passive than an event handler.

This doesn't prevent us from making an async dispatch if we really want to. Let's take a look at one example:

```
const [state, dispatch] = useState(1)
const onClick = () => {
  setTimeout(() => {
    dispatch(3)
  }, 0)
  dispatch(5)
}
```

In the preceding example, `setTimeout` is used to fire a callback in an async way. After the mouse click, `dispatch(5)` is invoked first. And after the update, `dispatch(3)` is invoked, even though the timeout duration is set to `0`.

Keep in mind, if you do that, you are not only running the callback in an async way, but you also break out of the React scheduling cycle. The reason you might want to do this is that there can be conflicts during DOM changes, for example, during drag-and-drop handling. In order to finish our code before making the state change, we can push the dispatch to the next *JavaScript* task queue.

6

Use Memo to Boost Performance

In the previous chapter, we learned how the `useEffect` hook is designed and how to use it to manage a side effect in *React*. In this chapter, we will change to an optimization topic for reusing the last assignment. We will first introduce how we can run into performance degradation in a typical web application. Then, we will walk through the design and source code behind `useMemo` and describe various ways of reusing a value conditionally. We'll then apply the optimization technique to two common cases: clicking to search and debouncing the search. At the end, the chapter also includes two bonus topics in the *Appendix* section, *Not a Classical Memorization* and *Skipping a Child Update*.

We will cover the following main topics in this chapter:

- Performance degradation
- Understanding the `useMemo` design
- Reusing a last assignment
- Test-Driving `useMemo`
- `useMemo` examples
- Questions and answers
- Appendix

Performance degradation

When we build a site, we normally start it with a draft or prototype version where a couple of pages are laid out with the sample data and the preliminary logic. The idea is to start small and see whether the site has any potential to grow. Though this is a very common approach, interestingly, most of the performance-related issues do not show up at this point. When the site with the real business logic grows, we start to experience performance degradation issues. Understanding how these issues are created in the first place is valuable since it helps us plan for the growth of the site.

Let's build such a case from scratch. A variable defined inside the body of a function component is evaluated when it gets invoked:

```
const Title = ({ text }) => {
  const a = 1
  ...
}
```

In the preceding code, the a variable is assigned with a 1 constant. Storing a number like this shouldn't cost us much when a is reassigned every time when the text prop changes. But what if we need to calculate something heavy, such as matching a text in a large array?

```
const Title = ({ text }) => {
  const found = matchTextInArray(text)
  ...
}
```

Say the preceding matchTextInArray function takes an average of 200 *milliseconds* to complete, which is a bit costly. We can argue that the found variable only gets assigned when text changes, so if text doesn't get changed often, we don't have to worry about found getting assigned too often. Let's ponder over this a bit.

A function component can be invoked for various reasons. In *React*, the update of a function component is mostly triggered by a state change. However, the state could be from inside the Title component or from the parent (or grandparent) of the Title component. Therefore, we can't just assume the update frequency of a component by looking at it.

Just imagine if the user decides to refresh the page; it should cause all the components of this page to update. In a way, the component can only determine what gets updated but can't entirely decide when it gets updated. In other words, when it comes to the update, the component also depends on its parent's behavior.

Let's take a look at the following example:

```
const Title = ({ text, flag }) => {
  const found = matchTextInArray(text)
  ...
}
```

In the preceding code, the `Title` component gets another `flag` prop. Thus, whenever the `flag` prop flips, it renders and spends 200 milliseconds on calculating a. You can imagine the flag as a user voting button from a parent component.

If the user keeps clicking the button, multiple 200 milliseconds can quickly stack up to become a second or two, and the performance of the app is essentially now tied directly to how quickly the user flips the flag. When this happens, to use a gaming term here, it causes a lag, or a frame drop. The user should start to feel a laggy response and lose confidence in using the site.

When this happens in a game, what do we do? Well, that's the time the gamer needs to upgrade their gaming hardware. But it could also be a time for developers to exploit an opportunity for optimization.

Reusing a previous assignment

So, what do we do in the situation of performance degradation? Let's take a look at what we have following the current timeline. When either the `flag` or the `text` prop changes, the `found` variable gets a new assignment:

```
|----TFTF--------TF------> flag flip
----------a---------b----> text change
c----cccc-c------cc-c----> new assignment
```

So, in our case, there's something we want to acknowledge, that is, the `matchTextInArray` does not even depend on the `flag` because the function doesn't take input arguments other than `text`.

Why do we want to perform a new assignment when the previous assignment could still be valid? Can't we skip assignments when the `flag` prop changes?

We learned in *Chapter 5, Use Effect to Handle Side Effects,* that an effect can be used to listen to a value change. In our case, can we listen to the `text` prop change to make an assignment while ignoring other values? Let's give it a shot:

```
const Title = ({ text, flag }) => {
  const [found, setFound] = useState("")
  useEffect(() => {
```

```
        setFound(matchTextInArray(text))
    }, [text])
    ...
}
```

In the preceding code, we use the dependency array from `useEffect` to act upon the `text` change and dispatch to update the `found` state after `matchTextInArray`. This is confirmed by the following timeline sketch:

```
|----TFTF--------TF------> flag flip
----------a---------b----> text change
-c---------c---------c---> new assignment
```

The solution works out of the box. The flag flips back and forth lots of times (six times), but we only have three new assignments due to the text change. Thus, the assignment isn't tied to the flip. This is wonderful because we manage to overcome potential performance degradation.

Though the solution works, we would like to improve upon it because it uses a side effect to handle the assignment, and we can see this assignment doesn't have to be a side effect. Since a side effect gets collected later after the update, it must wait till the next update. This means the assignment behaves very differently from a direct assignment, such as a = 1. Last but not least, a `found` state is used to hold the assignment value, and the value does not have to be a state. It's better if we can address all these issues.

React adds a `useMemo` hook to do exactly that without other hurdles. The job of the hook is to allow us to reuse the previous assignment in an update. Let's take a look at the `useMemo` design first.

Understanding the useMemo design

React provides a `useMemo` hook to support a value assignment through a function that can either return a new value or an old value from the previous update:

```
const Title = () => {
  const label = useMemo(() => {
    return "Hello World"
  }, [])
}
```

The `useMemo` function takes a `create` function as its first input argument. This function returns a new value if invoked. The second parameter is a `deps` dependency array, similar to `deps` in `useEffect`. In the preceding case, "Hello World" is assigned to a `label` variable only once after the mount.

There's no additional data structure required for useMemo other than the basic hook support, as shown in *Figure 6.1*:

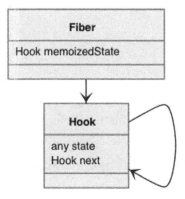

Figure 6.1 – Data structure for useMemo

The hook's state persists between updates, and it's up to each hook function to define what (or in which format) it wants to persist. For instance, a useState hook stores a state array, a useEffect hook stores an effect object, and now a useMemo hook stores things related to an assignment. In fact, useMemo takes the form of the assigned value and the dependency array as [value, deps].

The source code of useMemo is structured with mountMemo and updateMemo in a typical hook setup, depending on whether the fiber is under mount or the update via the isFiberMounting flag, as explained in *Chapter 3, Hooking into React*:

```
function useMemo(create, deps) {
  if (isFiberMounting) {
    return mountMemo(create, deps)
  } else {
    return updateMemo(create, deps)
  }
}
```

The useMemo hook accepts the create assignment function and the deps dependency array as inputs. The name, create, indicates that it creates a new value when it gets invoked.

When under the mount, it first gets the hook object by creating one:

```
function mountMemo(create, deps) {
  const hook = mountHook()
  const value = create()
  hook.state = [value, deps]
  return value
}
```

If deps is not given at all, it's converted to null by default, and the initial value is stored by invoking the create assignment function. Before returning the value, both the initial value and its dependency are stored in the state property under the hook using an array.

When under the update, it gets the hook by cloning one:

```
function updateMemo(create, deps) {
  const hook = updateHook()
  const prevState = hook.state
  if (prevState !== null) {
    if (deps !== null) {
      const prevDeps = prevState[1]
      if (areDepsEqual(ndeps, prevDeps)) {
        return prevState[0]
      }
    }
  }
  const value = create()
  hook.state = [value, deps]
  return value
}
```

Once we have the hook, it gets prevState from the hook's state, which is an array of the previous value and the previous dependency array.

It checks whether the dependency has changed with areDepsEqual. If there's no change, it simply returns the previous value. And if there is a change, it invokes the create assignment function again to update into the new value. Before we return the value, both the value and the dependency are stored in the hook's state. Here is the summarized useMemo workflow:

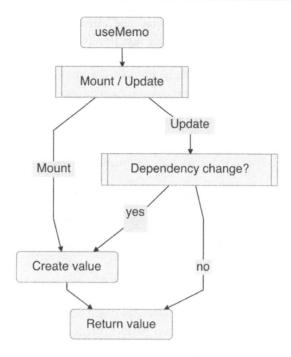

Figure 6.2 – useMemo workflow

Compared to `useState` and `useEffect`, `useMemo` is quite straightforward. It doesn't have any dispatch or effect involved. Instead, you can think of it as a special assignment statement. When the `deps` dependency is met, it then creates a value and returns it as the current value. In all cases, the current value is returned. So, to be precise, *an assignment is made in all cases; when the condition isn't met, an old value is reused.*

Now that we know how `useMemo` is designed, let's walk you through all the scenarios that this special assignment can do.

Reusing a last assignment

Reusing a value and memorizing a value sometimes refer to similar behavior. However, it's worth noting that the `useMemo` hook can only remember one value from the past, the last value.

A single *JavaScript* variable, by default, serves a purpose that, unless overwritten by a new assignment, holds the previously assigned value. So, take caution when reading the word "memo" here. If you take the word "memo" as a single value instead of memorizing all values, it could help you visualize it the right way as *React* designed it. If you are interested in classical memorization, check out the *Appendix A – Not a classical memorization* section at the end of this chapter.

How `useMemo` reuses the previous assignment is controlled by a `deps` dependency array, and it uses the `areDepsEqual` utility function to compare two dependency arrays between the previous and current update. We have already examined this function in *Chapter 5, Use Effect to Handle Side Effects*. We will skip the source code here and jump straight to the scenarios that correspond to each dependency array configuration.

Similarly, we get three cases here, no dependency, empty dependency, and some dependencies:

- **No dependency**:

  If the dependency array is omitted entirely, it creates a new value in every update:

  ```
  const v = useMemo(() => {...})
  ```

  This is rarely used in production because it's almost reverted to the direct assignment, as in the following:

  ```
  const v = ...
  ```

  The usage of `useMemo` without a dependency provided is not common, but it's easy to see how a `useMemo` hook statement and a direct assignment can replace each other very quickly, as they share the assignment statement in . . . .

- **Empty dependency**:

  If a `deps` array is provided but with no element inside, it means the value doesn't depend on anything. Therefore, the value is created only once after the mount:

  ```
  const v = useMemo(() => {...}, [])
  ```

  If you want to hold a static value for all updates, this is a good use of it. You might wonder why we can't take a static value declaration outside of the component. It's because the assignment can still use the variables inside the component.

- **Some dependencies**:

  This is the most popular usage of `useMemo`. When the elements of `deps` are not empty, it compares each element between the previous and next dependencies to determine the change:

  ```
  const v = useMemo(() => {...}, [a, b])
  ```

  If any of the elements change, the value gets assigned again.

There's one thing to make a note of – in all of the cases mentioned, the assignment is performed for all updates. Though sometimes the assignment seems to be skipped, what we really mean here is that the assignment is reused from the last time when the conditions met.

Assignment value type

The type of value that returns from the assignment can be in any format – a string, a number, an object, or even a function. That makes useMemo a bit flexible to meet all cases that require reusing values:

```
const a = useMemo(() => {
  return b + 3
}, [b])
```

The preceding usage of useMemo adds a 3 number to b and assigns the result to a when b changes. Similarly, we can construct a usage for using an object:

```
const obj = useMemo(() => {
  return { name }
}, [name])
```

In the preceding usage, an object with a name property is assigned to obj when name changes. We can even construct a usage for a function:

```
const fn = useMemo(() => {
  return () => {
    return 1
  }
}, [])
```

In the preceding code, we constructed an assignment to create a function instance after being mounted. To make things a bit easier to understand, we can take useMemo out to see what the raw assignment is:

```
const fn = () => { return 1 }
```

There's some subtlety when it comes to the usage of useMemo applying to a non-primitive value, such as an object, an array, or a function. When creating any of these values, you get a new value pointing to a new memory space. This means that when the dependency conditions are not met, old memory space is used instead.

All in all, the useMemo hook can be used as a special assignment to return any type of value.

The myth of skipping an update

We may all be thinking from the use of the word "memo" that, maybe, useMemo can help us skip an update:

```
const Title = () => {
  const a = useMemo(() => { ... }, [])
  return <Child a={a} />
}
```

In the preceding code, since the a variable doesn't get a new value after the mount, maybe the Child component doesn't get any new updates either. Unfortunately, this is not the case.

The answer to this question harks back to what makes an update in *React*. We mentioned at the beginning of this chapter that a state change from the Title component or its parent can make a new update, but the a variable is not a state and no one makes a dispatch for updating this value either.

In a way, the useMemo hook has no direct relationship with an update. It doesn't carry any functionalities in terms of hooking into the update as either useState or useEffect does. In fact, useMemo doesn't do anything more than an assignment, except the assignment is conditional.

Skipping an update based on the prop change can be done with a memo function provided by React. And memo and useMemo are two different things; we do not discuss memo in this book. If you really want to skip an update with the useMemo hook, we provide a special usage in the *Appendix B – Skipping a child update* section at the end of this chapter.

Now that we know what useMemo is and what it can and cannot do, let's give it a test drive.

Test-Driving useMemo

Let's improve the example that we saw at the beginning of the chapter with the useMemo hook to gain some performance:

```
const Title = ({ text, flag }) => {
  const found = useMemo(() => {
    console.log('created')              ①
    return matchTextInArray(text))
  }, [text])
  console.log('updated', found)         ②
  ...
}
```

The preceding code replaces useState and useEffect with useMemo. Let's take a look at the timeline to see what difference it makes:

```
|----TFTF--------TF------> flag
----------a---------b----> text
R----RRRR-R--------R----> updated ②
c---------c---------c----> created ①
```

A new value is created in the "created" series when the text changes, independent of the flag flips. Even better this time, there's no delay between assigning the found value and receiving the text change because it's a direct assignment under the same update now.

It's important to note that with or without useMemo, there's no big code structure change introduced to address the performance issue. In fact, to switch back to the non-optimized version, we can either omit the dependency or simply remove the useMemo usage with only one or two lines.

Okay, we have now seen how the useMemo hook is used. Next, let's take a look at two examples of how we can apply it to some real performance issues.

useMemo examples

The useMemo hook tends to be a hook that we use when we want to optimize the site for either resolving site performance and/or improving user experience. Thus, it normally tends to be used to address problems. In the following sections, we will go through two examples relating to a search to demonstrate the application of useMemo as an optimization tool.

Clicking to search

Say you have a list of fruits and you'd like to search it to find the matched fruit using an input box and a button. For example, typing "bl" should return us blackberries and blueberries from a list of fruits.

Figure 6.3 – Clicking on the search UI

Here's a list of fruits defined in a `fruits` global variable:

```
const fruits = ["Apple", "Banana", "Blackberries", ...]
```

We use a `text` state to store the string that the user types in at the moment. When the user clicks the **Search** button, the current `text` is sent to a `query` state as the current search query string:

```
const Title = () => {
  const [text, setText] = useState('')
  const [query, setQuery] = useState('')
  const matched = fruits.filter(v => v.includes(query))
  const onType = e => { setText(e.target.value) }
  const onSearch = () => { setQuery(text) }
  console.log('updated', text)         ②
  return (
    <>
      <input value={text} onChange={onType} />
      <button onClick={onSearch}>Search</button>
      {{matched.join(',')}}
    </>
  )
}
```

The `fruits` list is filtered against the `query` string to find our `matched` fruits. The preceding code works out of the box. But, after we send this piece to production, we get some feedback that the *UI* chokes a bit and can become quite laggy when a user types on the keyboard quickly or corrects their typos frequently.

As we dug into the issue, we found out that the problem is caused by the following line of code:

```
const matched = titles.filter(v => v.includes(query))
```

We can take a look at the timelines to help us visualize the problem:

```
|----kkkk--------kk------> user type
---------x---------x----> search click
R-----RRRR-R------RR-R---> updated   ②
m-----mmmm-m------mm-m---> created   ②
```

Every keystroke the user types translates into an update where the matched value is created. This is the exact same problem we talked about in our introduction, except that text and query are both states instead of props. The nature of the problem is the same though.

So, the solution here is to see whether we can limit the matched values to be created only upon the query change. This way, when the user types, we do not need to constantly make new matched values. Let's try this idea with useMemo:

```
const matched = useMemo(() => {
  console.log('created', query)    ①
  return titles.filter(v => v.includes(query))
}, [query])
```

Note that we added query to the deps change dependency array. If other things changed – for example, the user type – it shouldn't touch the matched values. Let's confirm it with the following timeline:

```
|----kkkk--------kk------> user type
----------x---------x----> search click
R-----RRRR-R------RR-R---> updated    ②
m----------m----------m---> created    ①
```

Now, we get a lower amount of new matched values, and the performance isn't tied to how the user types the keystroke anymore. This is great as we can all type quickly these days.

> **Playground – Click to Search**
>
> Feel free to play with this online example at https://codepen.io/ windmaomao/pen/OJjmjBv.

Click and search is one of the classic examples of user experience, and it serves as a solid pattern when it comes to performing a search on the web. While this approach is still being used, these days, users expect more from a responsive website, so there exists a more popular approach of improving the user experience with this problem.

Debouncing the search

We all have used *Google* to search for something at some point. When we type in the search bar, a dropdown slides down to provide the closest matches following the user input. It's a very smooth user experience, as *Google* has trained all of us to get used to it for decades, as shown in *Figure 6.4*:

Figure 6.4 – Debouncing the search UI

There's no search button the user can click anymore; all the user needs to do is to keep typing. And when the user stops typing, the matched list is revealed. So, how do we implement this? Let's first remove the **Search** button:

```
const Title = () => {
  const [text, setText] = useState('')
  const [query, setQuery] = useState('')
  const matched = useMemo(() => {
    console.log('created', query)      ①
    return fruits.filter(v => v.includes(query))
  }, [query])
  const onType = e => {
    const v = e.target.value
    setText(v)
    setQuery(v)
  }
  console.log('updated', text)         ②
  return (
    <>
      <input value={text} onChange={onType} />
      {matched.join(',')}
    </>
  )
}
```

Although we don't have the button to click, the nature of this click-to-search doesn't change. Somehow, we still need a moment of this "click" when the user is about to finish typing and expect a search to happen. So, the idea here is to find the right "click" moment.

How exactly can we know such timing, when something is about to happen but has not happened yet? Actually, there's a perfect analogy for this problem. Ever wondered how an elevator waits for all people to get inside before it closes its door? How does the door know when is the right time to close it? How does it anticipate whether no one else is going to get squeezed in at the next second?

Given an `fn` function, if a request to invoke it arrives, it doesn't do it right away. Instead, it waits for a certain amount of time. During that period, if no request comes in to invoke it anymore, it then invokes at the end of the period. This behavior is called **Debouncing**.

Debouncing was introduced for mechanical switches and relays – coincidence? To resolve hitting the key too frequently, the processor in a keyboard defers the hitting by "combining" them across time into a single hit. Quite a few libraries implement the `debounce` function; instead of reinventing the wheel, this book borrows one from a library called *Lodash*:

```
const debouncedFn = debounce(fn, dt)
```

The `debounce` function takes the original `fn` function and a `dt` duration to wait before invoking `fn`; it returns a new `debouncedFn` function with the debouncing behavior. Instead of invoking `fn`, we invoke `debouncedFn` now.

Let's apply it to find the right moment of "click":

```
const setDebouncedQuery = debounce(
  t => { setQuery(t) }, 300
)
const onType = e => {
  const v = e.target.value
  setText(v)
  setDebouncedQuery(v)
}
```

In the preceding change, upon each user typing, a debounced `setDebouncedQuery` version gets invoked. But not all typing updates the query via `setQuery`; instead, it waits 300 *milliseconds* to make sure the user happens to stop the typing, and that moment is our moment of "click." Multiple user keystrokes are combined into a single `setQuery`. As we have set up, after each `query` change, the `useMemo` hook creates a new search.

There's only one small issue left to get everything working; the `setDebouncedQuery` function is created as a new instance upon each user keystroke, which is not what we wanted. Instead, we want to have one instance of `setDebouncedQuery` so that all the keystrokes can be debounced to the same `setQuery` function. How do we reuse the last function instance? Yes – with the `useMemo` hook we just learned about:

```
const setDebouncedQuery = useMemo(() => {
  return debounce(t => {
    console.log('clicked')            ③
    setQuery(t))
  }, 300)
}, [setQuery])
```

In the preceding code, we improved `setDebouncedQuery` with the usage of the `useMemo` hook, and inside we inserted `debounce` for `setQuery`. Now, let's confirm with the following timeline:

```
|----kkkk--------kk------> user type
---------x---------x-----> "clicked" ③
R-----RRRRR-------RRR----> updated   ②
m--------m---------m----> created    ①
```

Awesome! For two groups of user sessions, it performs two searches. Comparing this timeline with the previous timeline as in the classical clicking to search, you can see they are quite similar. The physical button click is replaced with an imaginary "click," and we get a nicer user experience.

> **Playground – Debouncing the Search**
>
> Feel free to play with this online example at `https://codepen.io/windmaomao/pen/xxLdPga`.

With these two examples, we should now know how `useMemo` can be applied effectively.

Summary

In this chapter, we first learned about a new hook, `useMemo`. We first briefly went over what can cause performance degradation in general, and then we learned about the `useMemo` design and read line by line how an optimization scheme is constructed to reuse the last value without creating a new one every time. Then, we went through all scenarios of reusing a value based on a dependency array. We took `useMemo` for a spin, and at the end, we saw how it's applied to two classic examples, clicking to search and debouncing the search.

In the next chapter, we will get into another hook in the *React* family where a state change can be dispatched to multiple locations for an are update.

Questions

Here are some questions and answers to refresh your knowledge:

1. What is useMemo?

    A useMemo hook is an assignment statement where a new value is created when one of the dependencies changes. It can be used to minimize the creation of a value, so it behaves like that sometimes when an assignment is "skipped."

2. What's the common usage of useMemo?

    It's mainly used as an optimization to avoid heavy operation on every render otherwise. If a certain evaluation is excessively used, thus blocking the *UI*, it is the right time to think about using useMemo to limit the usage to only relevant conditions. For instance, if typing isn't related to that task, we can take it out of the dependency list.

3. How do you use useMemo for memorization?

    useMemo doesn't remember all past values and only remembers the last created value. So, the best usage of it is to use it as a special assignment replacement, instead of a caching mechanism.

Appendix

Appendix A – Not a Classical Memorization

It's very easy to confuse useMemo with a **Memorization** used in computer science, as the name indicates.

Memorization is an optimization technique in computer programs, primarily designed to speed up the process by storing the results of expensive operations and returning the cached result if it has been computed under the same condition before. The last part, "under the same condition before," is the part that makes it special.

The *Fibonacci* sequence is a classical memorization problem. If it's written using a recursive algorithm, it can be very costly; therefore, we tend to use cache storage to store all past calculated values:

```
const fibs = { 0: 1, 1: 1 }
function fib(n)  {
  if (!fibs[n]) {
    fibs[n] = fibs[n - 1] + fibs[n - 2]
  }
  return fibs[n]
}
```

The preceding code gives a specialized fib function; if you call it sequentially from 1, 2, and so on, it can give you the next number without too much effort.

Say in the *React* app, we start with n=0; unless n moves to the next number, we don't want to calculate a new value. We could add useMemo:

```
const Title = ({ n, text }) => {
  const f = useMemo(() => fib(n), [n])
  return <div>{text} - {f}</div>
}
```

The first thing we quickly find out is that it actually reuses the fib function, which means their functionalities don't overlap at all. In another way, useMemo doesn't do what fib does. Amazing!

Another discovery is that what the Title component does is to ensure that when another text prop changes, it doesn't calculate f again. But if we change n from 3 to 2, it still creates
a new number. This means the code can be reduced to the following:

```
const Title = ({ n, text }) => {
  const f = fib(n)
  return <div>{text} - {f}</div>
}
```

Haha, this is a bit funny now. We literally removed useMemo. Why? Because the saved calculation is already implemented by fib, the classical memorization. Moreover, the useMemo hook doesn't provide any of that kind of storage.

useMemo has one memoized storage built for *a last value*. If you can take advantage of this, that's great. Otherwise, you just over-complicate things.

Don't expect useMemo to give you more values, since it doesn't even have a key/value map for multiple values. *React* itself is a big state machine; given a change, it moves to a new state. All it cares about is the current and next scene it's going into. Moving from t-1 to t is what *React* is good at, but not at moving from t to t-2. Therefore, useMemo can't fit in the memorization context, which is normally what caching is about.

Appendix B – Skipping a Child Update

We will use a profiler chart provided by *React Developer Tools* to inspect the React component hierarchies inside the browser, as shown in *Figure 6.5*:

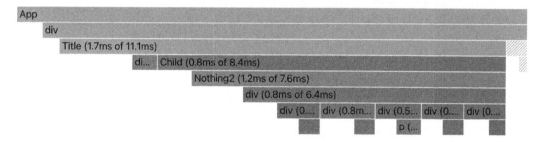

Figure 6.5 – Profiler render with Child bailout failed

What a profiler chart provides is a topology overview of all the fibers visited in one update. The topology speaks for itself on how they are wired like a tree. Moreover, we can tell what happened to them based on their colors.

A bar with a solid color stands for an update from this component. On the other hand, if the color is shaded gray, it means that *React* decides to skip updating the component, termed as a bailout.

The chart is useful when we get to study the performance of the site because it can tell us in a given update how many fibers are replaced and how many are reused, and whether a particular fiber has been visited or not.

A value created by useMemo can be used for any purpose. For it to impact a child component, it can be wired with a prop to send the info deeper:

```
const Title = () => {
  const a = useMemo(() => { ... }, [])
  return <Child a={a} />
}
```

If we get a previous assignment of the a variable wiring to the Child component via a prop, does that mean we can have a conditional update of Child? This is a good question.

From the profiler chart corresponding to all components when the Title updates (see *Figure 6.5*), we quickly find out the answer is no. The preceding code can't make a skip of the Child update because, when the Title parent updates, it generates a new set of props through the reconciliation of the Child fiber. In other words, it triggers the update of Child regardless of whether an individual prop, such as a, has a new value.

Then, how exactly can we use useMemo to skip a child update manually? Let's try something different. Keep in mind what useMemo is designed to do – to hold a value from the last update until the condition is met again:

```
const Title = () => {
  const child = useMemo(() => {
    return <Child a="Hello World" />
  }, [])
  return child
}
```

In the preceding useMemo code, instead of returning a string, we use it to hold the <Child /> component instance. What is <Child />? It's an element object returned from the Child function component. So, as long as the element stays the same, we expect the screen to be the same. Let's confirm this approach with the profiler chart, as shown in *Figure 6.6*:

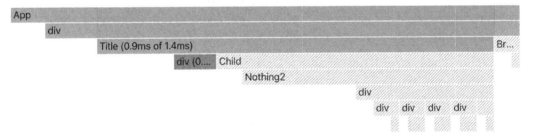

Figure 6.6 – Profiler render with Child bailout successful

After the mount, as the [] dependency array indicates, child holds the same Child update from the last time. Now, when the Title component gets updated, it doesn't update the Child component. This is because, to React, there's no dispatched change from under the Title component, so it bails out everything underneath it.

7
Use Context to Cover an Area

In the previous chapter, we learned how `useMemo` is designed and how to use `useMemo` to conditionally reuse the last value. In this chapter, we will talk about how to propagate changes to cover an area update. We will introduce what an area update is and how *React* context is used to share a value within that area. Then, we will walk through the data structure and source code behind `useContext` to consume the shared value. And finally, we'll provide two practical examples of applying contexts to the theme and the table. The chapter also includes two bonus topics in the *Appendix* section: *Propagating a context* and *Context scope and value*.

We will cover the following topics in this chapter:

- What is an area update?
- Introducing the React context
- Understanding the `useContext` design
- Test driving `useContext`
- `useContext` examples
- Questions and answers
- Appendix

What is an area update?

On a typical website, once the site is loaded, it starts listening to all user actions. Each action received gets handled on a first-come, first-served basis. Normally, the impact of each action is limited to one small region of the screen, using a *UI* term, a single component. However, sometimes, a user action can do more than that.

Let's use the computer as an analogy. Say you decide to change the color settings of your system. Once the color is changed, the computer goes through all the open windows and applies that color to them. Therefore, this action can impact multiple applications spread across the screen. This becomes an area update.

Have you wondered how we can make an area update when the impacted components are located very distantly from each other? To be able to answer this question, let's first recall a single update introduced in *Chapter 4, Use State to Jumpstart Components*.

A fiber tree is scheduled for a single update upon receiving an action. This update is localized around a source fiber where the action is received (the red dot in *Figure 7.1*). *React* follows the source and collects all the changes associated with it and then applies them to the *DOM* (red lines). This is the single update pattern in *React*.

Figure 7.1 – A single update originating from a user action

Say the source fiber is a `Title` component:

```
const Title = () => {
  const [count, dispatch] = useState(0)
  const onClick = () => {
    dispatch(count + 1)
  }

  return (
    <>
      <div onClick={onClick}>{count}</div>
      ...
```

```
      </>
   )
}
```

The preceding `Title` component gets updated when the user clicks on `count`. It should also update other children in the . . . section.

Now, consider another component called `ThumbUp`:

```
const ThumbUp = () => {
   // made up count
   return count > 5 ? "Awesome" : ""
}
```

The intention of the `ThumbUp` component is to respond to `count`. When it becomes greater than 5, we want an `"Awesome"` message to be printed on the screen. The `ThumbUp` component is located in *Figure 7.2*:

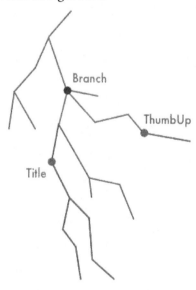

Figure 7.2 – Two updates responding to a single user action

Currently, the `count` variable in the `ThumbUp` component is a made-up one because we don't know how it can be passed from the `Title` component. All we know is that we want to share this `count` among both components and the challenge somehow lies in their relationship.

Apparently, these two components are not a child or parent to one another. There's no direct path from one to the other unless we first go upward multiple steps to the Branch component (dark dot in *Figure 7.2*) and then go down again picking another route. Essentially, Branch is their common ancestor. So how exactly can we send information between two nodes that are not in a direct parent/child relationship?

Let's explore this question by taking two approaches, starting with the props approach.

Props approach

Since the React props only work for the parent/child setup, to apply the props to this problem, we need to promote the relevant state to a common ancestor, the Branch component:

```
const Branch = () => {
    const [count, dispatch] = useState(0)
    const onClick = () => {
      dispatch(count + 1)
    }

    return (
      <>
        <div>
          . . .
            <Title count={count} onClick={onClick} />
          . . .
        </div>
        <div>
          . . .
            <ThumbUp count={count} />
          . . .
        </div>
      </>
    )
}
```

In the preceding code, the count state is relocated from Title to Branch. From there, count and dispatch are then sent to the (distant) children via props. Now, if the state changes, the Branch component updates all its children, including Title and ThumbUp. OK, we managed to share the count state.

Although the props approach works in general, it does require us to modify the props for both the Title and ThumbUp components. Since there can be other components in the path between Branch and each of them, all components along the way need to be modified as well. Considering a typical site build, the need to share a state happens in the later stage of the project cycle. Taking this approach can be very expensive due to the number of components we need to modify.

So, is there a better way of sharing the prop without touching so many components? Looking at *Figure 7.2*, an intuitive approach could be to dispatch an update to the Title component, and an update to the ThumbUp component at the same time. The combined impact could produce an area update covering both. Let's see if we can make this idea work.

Combined dispatch approach

To have a combined dispatch, we need to allow both dispatches to be accessible from an event handler. This is a bit tricky since a dispatch function provided via useState is normally defined inside one component, either Title or ThumbUp. To get around that, let's say we use a global variable for now:

```
let dispatch2

const ThumbUp = () => {
  const [count, dispatch] = useState(0)
  dispatch2 = dispatch

  return count > 5 ? "Awesome" : ""
}
```

In the preceding code, we amended the ThumbUp component and added a count state and a dispatch function. We then used a global variable, dispatch2, to point to this dispatch function so that it can be invoked by other components. Now, with this change, we can ask the Title component to perform both dispatches:

```
const Title = () => {
  const [count, dispatch] = useState(0)
  const onClick = () => {
    dispatch(v => v + 1)
    dispatch2(v => v + 1)
  }

  return <div onClick={onClick}>{count}</div>
}
```

From the preceding setup, after the user clicks on `count`, it performs the `dispatch` from `Title` and performs `dispatch2` from `Greeting`. Although the two `count` states in each component are not pointing to a shared value, both are incremented respectively from these two dispatches. *React* batches these two dispatches into one update to the screen, and if the user continues clicking the number, you will see an `"Awesome"` message on the screen when the `count` state gets bigger than 5.

You might not believe this hack-ish approach would work, but it does. The fact that we call a dispatch function for another component is a bit beyond what *React* designs `useState` to do, but it's not incorrect. This approach requires fewer changes to the code structure. There's no prop involved. All changes are made on the local side of `Title` and `ThumbUp`. More importantly, it serves as an educational case that an update impacting multiple components can be composed of multiple updates.

OK, what we learned from these two approaches is that we want to avoid passing props all the way down in this non-parent/child case, and we want to share the value as well as trigger a sort of combined update following the value change. Moreover, in practice, if the solution can provide the joint dispatch out of the box and require minor modifications to the existing code structure, that would be even better.

By the end of 2017, the *React* team found such needs and introduced a new version of context to address its current limitations at that time. What the new context does is that it helps to share a value through multiple levels of components without requiring a prop in each level. It also provides a mechanism for a distant child component to access a value from an ancestor component. Let's take a look at this *React* context.

Introducing the React context

The context is modeled with a `ReactContext` data type holding a `_currentValue` value.

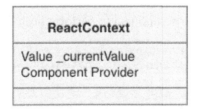

Figure 7.3 – React context data structure

We can create a context with the `createContext` function. For instance, if we want to share a piece of user info, we can create a `UserContext` and hold a `defaultValue`:

```
const UserContext = createContext(defaultValue)

export default UserContext
```

The created context can be shared via a *JavaScript* `export` statement, and this way, when any other file or component needs it, it can be imported.

The context allows us to provide the value to all consumers underneath via a `Provider` property:

```
import UserContext from './UserContext'

const Branch = () => {
  return (
    <UserContext.Provider value={...}>
    ...
    </UserContext.Provider>
  )
}
```

A context provider, such as `UserContext.Provider`, accepts a `value` prop to share. The provider is a special component. Unlike a function component, it has its own update implementation. When it gets updated due to a change in `value`, it kicks off a search.

The search goes through its children, and its children's children recursively, until everything under gets visited. For all consumers using the context, they are marked to be updated. If you are interested in knowing more about the context provider, check out *Appendix A – Propagating a context*, at the end of this chapter.

Hence, a provider's job is to share a value. If multiple values of different purposes are required, we can stack them together. Let's say that, on top of `UserContext`, we have one more `ThemeContext` context to share:

```
const Branch = ({ user, theme }) => {
  return (
    <ThemeContext.Provider value={theme}>
      <UserContext.Provider value={user}>
        ...
      </UserContext.Provider>
    </ThemeContext.Provider>
  )
}
```

The preceding usage would enable any consumer in the . . . section to read the value from theme or user, or both.

One interesting aspect regarding the design of the provider is that a provider can be nested under the same provider to override the shared value:

```
const Branch = ({ theme1, theme2 }) => {
  return (
    <ThemeContext.Provider value={theme1}>
      // A. value = theme1
      <ThemeContext.Provider value={theme2}>
        // B. value = theme2
      </ThemeContext.Provider>
      // C. value = theme1
    </ThemeContext.Provider>
    // D. value = defaultTheme
  )
}
```

In the preceding code, theme1 and theme2 are provided by two providers from the same ThemeContext definition. So, which context value does a consumer see, you might wonder?

There are four locations marked A, B, C, and D in the preceding code. The value a consumer sees depends on where it's consumed. For location A, the value a consumer sees is theme1, for location B, it's theme2, and for location C, it's back to theme1 again.

Essentially, the context provider is designed (in a way) like a *JavaScript* function. You can get different values in the different function scopes. To figure out the correct value at a particular location, you need to find the first ancestor parent that provides the value. The closest ancestor provider should provide the right context value. This should explain why location C gets theme1 instead of theme2.

Then what is the context value outside of any provider scope, for instance, at location D? Since it does not happen to be an ancestor provider that you can find above the Branch component. This is where defaultValue comes into play:

```
const ThemeContext = React.createContext(defaultTheme)
```

When no other provider can be found to provide the value, it takes the `defaultValue` supplied at the time the context is created. This implies that the default value isn't a must-have, but it can be useful for taking a sneak peek into the format of a context type early on:

```
const defaultTheme = {
  mode: 'light'
}
```

Internally, *React* uses a stack to push and pop the context to keep track of context values for all provider scopes. If you are interested in knowing this detail, check out *Appendix B – Context scope and value*, at the end of this chapter.

OK, now that we know how to provide a context value, let's see how we can consume it in a consumer/child component. *React* provides a `useContext` hook to do just that.

Understanding the useContext design

React provides a `useContext` hook to consume a context:

```
import UserContext from './UserContext'

const Title = () => {
  const user = useContext(UserContext)
  return <div>{user.name}</div>
}
```

The `useContext` hook function takes one input argument, `context`, and returns the shared value. `context` is normally imported from a definition file.

useContext data structure

We are going to explain how useContext is designed with a stripped-down version of the source code. Let's take a look at the data structure that makes it happen:

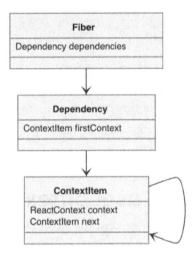

Figure 7.4 – useContext hook data structure

To consume (or read) a context value, each fiber gets a new dependencies property to keep track of all the context it consumes. This is because a component can use multiple useContext and each usage consumes a different context, such as UserContext and ThemeContext.

The dependencies property is designed as a linked list with its firstContext property to hold the first context with a ContextItem type. Each ContextItem holds a ReactContext (the context introduced earlier) and a next property pointing to the next context. The dependencies list is how the provider finds all consumers while propagating the update.

The useContext hook is designed to read a context value for all updates:

```
function useContext(context) {
  const contextItem = {
    context: context,
    next: null,
  }
  if (lastDependency === null) {
    lastDependency = contextItem
    updatingFiber.dependencies = {
      firstContext: contextItem,
    }
```

```
  } else {
    lastDependency =
      lastDependency.next = contextItem
  }
  ...
}
```

The main job of useContext in the preceding code block is to return _currentValue from context. It also appends context to the fiber's dependencies list before returning the context value.

lastDependency is an auxiliary variable that keeps track of the last context of the update. If this is the first context, it's then created as firstContext, otherwise it is appended to the next of the list. At the beginning of the update, lastDependency is set to be null. Thus, the list of dependencies for each fiber is recreated in every update, and this reminds us how hooks are created in each update.

useContext workflow

You have gone through a stripped-down version of useContext code. Here is the summary workflow for both provider and useContext:

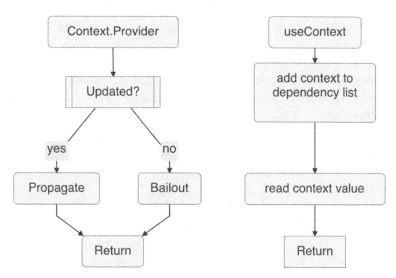

Figure 7.5 – useContext and ContextProvider workflow

Let's have a quick run-through. A context is provided through a provider. In the event of a value change from the provider, it finds all the consumers and propagates the update. Otherwise, it skips the update.

In an update, when a `useContext` hook is invoked with a given context, it appends the context to the fiber's `dependencies` list and returns the context's current value.

Now that we have gone through the overall design, let's take it all out for a test drive.

Test driving useContext

Context is fun to use and has quite a few common applications. Consider a site with a user logo displayed at the top-right corner of the screen:

Figure 7.6 – An application with App, Header, and Logo

The site is created with an `App` component, containing `Header` and `Main`. And in turn, `Header` contains `Logo`, and `Site` contains `Greeting`. App, `Header`, and `Logo` are defined as follows:

```
function App({ initialUser }) {
  const user = initialUser

  return (
    <div>
      <Header user={user} />
      <Main user={user} />
    </div>
  )
}

const Header = ({ user }) => {
  return <Logo user={user} />
}
```

```
const Logo = ({ user }) => {
  return (
    <div>
      <img url={ user.imageUrl } />
      <span>{ user.username }</span>
    </div>
  )
}
```

Assuming the user gets authenticated as an `initialUser` and sent to the App, it gets passed via a prop to `Header` and `Logo`. In `Logo`, it gets consumed by its `imageUrl` property and `username` to display a logo. Notice the interface for all components needs to carry `user` as a prop. Since we want to display a greeting message under `Main`, the `user` needs to be passed via a prop as well.

Let's see how a context can help to simplify this setup. Let's say we define a `UserContext`:

```
const UserContext = React.createContext()
export default UserContext
```

In the App, we can provide the `initialUser` via `UserContext.Provider`:

```
import UserContext from './UserContext'
const App = ({ initialUser }) => {
  const [user, changeUser] = useState(initialUser)
  const value = { user, changeUser }
  return (
    <UserContext.Provider value={value}>
      <div>
        <Header />
        <Site />
      </div>
    </UserContext.Provider>
  )
}
```

Notice that `Header` and `Main` don't have to carry the `user` prop anymore.

The App component creates a `user` state for holding `initialUser`. The `changeUser` function can be used to replace the current user if needed. It then assembles a `value` object from `user` and `changeUser` to be shared via `UserContext.Provider`.

Inside `Logo`, we can consume the value provided, which includes the `user` property:

```
import UserContext from './UserContext'
const Logo = () => {
  const { user } = useContext(UserContext)
  return (
    <div>
      <img url={ user.imageUrl } />
      <span>{ user.username }</span>
    </div>
  )
}
```

In the preceding code, the `user` object is obtained by reading off the `UserContext` via an ES6 syntax. For those readers who are interested in knowing about ES6 usages, check out the *Embracing JavaScript ES6* section in *Chapter 10, Building a Website with React*. Once the `user` is obtained, we can use the `imageUrl` and `username` properties of `user` to quickly wire them to the existing `Logo` component.

The same applies to the components under `Main`, such as `Greeting`, which shows the `Hello Fang` message depending on the currently logged-in user. We can utilize the context to accomplish that with little effort:

```
import UserContext from './UserContext'

const Greeting = () => {
  const { user } = useContext(UserContext)
  return <h1>Hello {user.username}</h1>
}
```

It's important to note that with a context such as `UserContext`, our app becomes much more manageable and scalable pertaining to everything about accessing the `user` object. Because the information becomes context info, as long as the component falls into this context, it can access it.

Now that we know how to read the user object, let's see if we can change it from `initialUser`, such as allowing the user to log in and out of the app.

Changing the context value

Say we add a **Logout** button under `Logo`. When this button is clicked, the current user is logged out, meaning their logo should no longer be available for display:

```
import UserContext from './UserContext'
const Logo = () => {
```

```
  const { user, changeUser } = useContext(UserContext)
  const { imageUrl, username } = user
  const authenticated = username != undefined
  const onLogout = () => { changeUser({}) }
  const onLogin = () => { // redirect to LoginForm }
  return (
    <div>
      {authenticated ? (
        <>
          <img url={ imageUrl } />
          <span>{ username }</span>
          <button onClick={onLogout}>Logout</button>
        </>
      ) : (
          <button onClick={onLogin}>Login</button>
      )}
    </div>
  )
}
```

In the preceding code, the changeUser function is provided via UserContext. It defines an authenticated flag based on whether the username is available. This flag can be used to decide whether the *UI* should display the **Logout** or **Login** button.

If the user is authenticated, the **Logout** button is displayed. Upon clicking, the onLogout event handler is triggered to changeUser to an empty object, {}. changeUser is a dispatch function we defined earlier, and when it updates the user, it also propagates the update to all consumers, including the Logo component. Thus, when the next update arrives, user holds an empty object with no username.

If the user is not authenticated, the **Login** button is then displayed. Upon clicking, the onLogin event handler is triggered where we can redirect the user to a LoginForm (the redirection code is omitted here):

```
const LoginForm = () => {
  const { changeUser } = useContext(UserContext)
  const onSubmit = (_user) => {
    changeUser(_user)
    // redirect to home page
  }
  return ...
}
```

LoginForm also consumes the UserContext and reads the changeUser property. Upon successful submission of the form, we can use changeUser again to change the empty user into an authenticated user. Similarly, the new update propagates the update to all consumers, including Logo and Greeting. Thus, the user will see their logo and username in the top-right corner after logging in, as well as a greeting message on the main body. See *Figure 7.6*.

User login and logout are generally important operations for a site because it has a direct impact on site authentication and authorization. Especially when refreshing the page entirely isn't an option, the context is a perfect fit in terms of reading and writing the user object without worrying about the out-of-sync moment among various components.

Now that we have seen how a context update orchestrates the updating of all components in the event of a context change, let's take a look at two more examples using contexts in real applications.

useContext examples

Context is used for sharing site-wise information, but it can be also very effective in sharing things in a narrower area. In this section, we'll see examples of both cases.

Theme context

One nice and common usage involving a context is theming, which allows the user to switch between a light and dark theme based on their preference. See *Figure 7.7*:

Figure 7.7 – A theme made with light and dark options

To implement this feature, let's start with ThemeContext:

```
const ThemeContext = React.createContext({
  mode: 'light',  // or 'dark'
})
```

We can set the default theme with an object supporting a mode property, which is a string to hold either "light" or "dark".

Design theme context

Any component that requires the theme can read the settings from `ThemeContext`. Let's build a theme-aware `Button` component:

```
const Button = () => {
  const theme = useContext(ThemeContext)
  return (
    <ButtonStyle mode={theme.mode}>
     Ok
    </ButtonStyle>
}
```

We can theme the button's style based on the shared `mode` inside the `ButtonStyle` component:

```
const color = props =>
  props.mode === 'light' : 'black' ? 'white'
const ButtonStyle = styled.button`
  color: ${color};
`
```

`ButtonStyle` is a styled component applied on top of the host `button` component with modified *CSS*. It receives the `mode` prop and, based on that, we can define its `color` with either `"white"` or `"black"`. If you are interested in using `StyledComponent`, please check out the *Adopting CSS-in-JS approach* section of *Chapter 10, Building a Website with React*.

Based on this approach, we can build lots of other theme-aware components. And imagine a situation where we have a couple of them under `App`; in the event of the mode changing, they can all be flipped to their corresponding styles in a single update:

```
const App = ({ theme }) => {
  return (
    <ThemeContext.Provider value={theme}>
      ...
    </ThemeContext.Provider>
}
```

Now let's talk about how to design a context. In the preceding theming case, we used `mode` to flip between themes, but we also can bake the exact style into it:

```
const ThemeContext = React.createContext({
  primaryColor: 'blue',
  secondaryColor: 'red'
})
```

In the preceding context, two individual colors for primary and secondary purposes are defined. This way, we can directly read the color in `Button`:

```
const color = props => props.primaryColor
const ButtonStyle = styled.button`
  color: ${color};
`
```

There's no right or wrong in terms of how we should design a context. The decision as to what property you should use is more or less based on how you want to consume these properties and design the components. In our case, the decision is more about whether the component should be based on `mode` or `primaryColor`.

Apply theme manually

Using a theme for a group of components works out great with a theme context. However, sometimes there will be a requirement where we want to apply a theme to one particular component without touching the theme of all the other components. This normally applies to a nav header component that gets a different contrast color to the rest of the site.

This problem can be solved by applying a context in a separate scope:

```
const Header = () => {
  return (
    <ThemeContext.Provider value={{ mode: 'dark' }}>
      <Button />
    </ThemeContext.Provider>
  )
}
```

In the preceding `Header` component, another usage of `ThemeContext.Provider` is written to provide a different `mode` theme, while `App` has already been provided with a `mode` theme. Let's say the `App` theme is `'light'`; it changes to `'dark'` when it enters `Header`.

When the theme-aware `Button` component gets updated, it looks for the closest ancestor that defines the provider. Since the ancestor found is `Header` instead of `App`, it reads the `'dark'` mode.

We are free to override parts of the context value instead of overriding the entire value:

```
const Header = () => {
  const theme = useContext(ThemeContext)
  const value = { ...theme, primaryColor: 'blue' }
  return (
    <ThemeContext.Provider value={value}>
```

```
        . . .
    </ThemeContext.Provider>
  )
}
```

In the preceding context, `Header` takes the current theme from the parent scope and overrides the `primaryColor` property to `'blue'`. Thus, all child consumers under `Header` see a modified theme setting.

> **Playground – Theme Context**
>
> Feel free to play with this online example at `https://codepen.io/windmaomao/pen/xxLrwJy`.

Now we see that a context is a perfect fit for site-wise subjects such as a theme. The context does not have to always be as big as a site; if we can identify an area, we should be able to apply a context to it. Let's take a look at an example where we apply the context to a targeted area such as a table.

Table context

Another usage of context is to apply the context to a place that can be small but big enough to contain many relevant components inside, such as a table. See *Figure 7.8*:

Figure 7.8 – A table containing customizable cell displays

A table can be quite complex in a modern *UI*, where it contains a header, a body, a footer, pagination, and a customizable column setting to drive the look and feel of cells. Moreover, all these elements can be assembled in a mix-and-match way on the fly to suit different business purposes.

Customizing table cells

A table is made up of rows and columns of cells where each cell can be controlled by a cell component such as `DefaultCell`:

```
const DefaultCell = ({ value }) => {
  return <div>{value}</div>
}
```

The prop `value` is used to pass in a primitive value from a property of a row, such as a string or a number. In a typical case, we simply display it as a string format, as in the preceding code.

Given a table row tracking a list of fruits:

```
const fruits = [
  { title: 'Apple', status: true },
  { title: 'Orange', },
  { title: 'Strawberry' },
  { title: 'Pineapple', status: true },
  { title: 'Watermelon' }
]
```

The preceding column for `title` is a perfect example, and it should display a list of fruit names. However, not all cells are plain strings, since we can display a cell as a status indicator, a progress bar, a checkbox, and so on. In our case, we have a column for `status` indicating whether the fruit tastes nice or just OK, which can be handled by another cell behavior:

```
const StatusCell = ({ value }) => {
  const s = value ? 'Nice' : 'Ok'
  return <div>{s}</div>
}
```

In the preceding custom `StatusCell` component, the value passed in is a boolean, and it displays either `'Nice'` or `'Ok'`.

This means we need a generic `TableCell` where we can pass in some sort of column information to customize the display:

```
const TableCell = ({ col, row }) => {
  const value = row[col.name]
  const Component = col.Cell || DefaultCell
  return <Component value={value} />
}
```

In the preceding `TableCell` component, a `col` prop is provided to describe how a cell should update. Let's take a look at the information in two columns for both `title` and `status`:

```
const cols = [
  { name: 'title' },
  { name: 'status', Cell: StatusCell }
]
```

For the second column, the `Cell` property is specified as a custom `StatusCell`, whereas the first column omits it, thus taking the `DefaultCell`. With this `col` capability, we can design a custom look and feel for all sorts of cells.

Design table context

The example so far displays the cell based on the cell content, `row[col.name]`. As long as the column name matches the data stored in the row data, we should find the correct cell value. But sometimes, they might not match or, even worse, sometimes we need to display a cell based on multiple columns. For instance, to display a person's full name, we need the person's first name and last name, which are spread out across two columns. Only `row` can provide enough. But we only have a cell `value`. Where can we get a `row`?

We can pass the `row` into each `TableCell` as a prop. But say we want to avoid the props approach to keep the cell interface flexible. In this case, we can create a `TableContext`:

```
const TableContext = React.createContext({
  rows: [],
  cols: [],
  row: {}
})

export default TableContext
```

In the preceding `TableContext`, we add a `row` property as well as `rows` and `cols` so that all consumers can share them. We can then provide it to each row of a table in the `TableRow` component:

```
import TableContext from './TableContext'

const TableRow = ({ row }) => {
  const table = useContext(TableContext)
  const value = { ...table, row }
  const cols = table.cols

  return (
```

```
    <TableContext.Provider value={value}>
      <TableRowStyle>
        {cols.map(col => {
          <TableCell
            row={row}
            col={col}
          />
        })}
      </TableRowStyle>
    </TableContext.Provider>
  )
}
```

The `TableRow` component is responsible for updating a row of the table. We use `TableContext` for two purposes here, one to get all the `cols` stored, and one to override the `row` property with one provided before providing the context back to each row. Now, when we get to each cell component, we should be able to get the current `row`. To demo it, we can set up another custom column for `'combo'`:

```
const cols = [
  { name: 'title' },
  { name: 'status', Cell: StatusCell },
  { name: 'combo', Cell: ComboCell }
]
```

The idea of the `'combo'` column is to join both `'title'` and `'status'` in a single cell via a custom `ComboCell` component:

```
const ComboCell = () => {
  const { row } = useContext(TableContext)
  const s = row.status ? 'Nice' : 'Ok'

  return <div>{row.title} - {s}</div>
}
```

In the preceding code, we grab the current `row` info from `TableContext` and access both the `title` and `status` properties. With this approach, we can literally assemble any information from the current row. Also, notice that there's no props passed into this component. This means, as long as you import `TableContext`, you can design a custom cell anywhere you want. This decoupling, having no explicit dependency, should make us very comfortable designing a custom cell style on the fly.

We can argue, were we to provide the `row` directly to the `ComboCell`, we would achieve the same functionalities without the table context setup. That can be true. The choice of whether you pass the `row` as a prop or from a context impacts how you design the cells.

In our case, passing `row` from a context does make the design a bit more flexible. Let's continue our example and see the usage of this `TableContext` in other places. Let's say this time that a cell needs to know more information, such as the `cols` settings, or even a piece of action associated with the table, such as deleting a row.

Let's take a look at one example where we delete a row of tables by clicking from a cell. Now, in order to manage the content of the table, we can provide a state `[rows, setRows]` to the `Table` component:

```jsx
const Table = ({ cols, rows, setRows }) => {
  const value = { cols, rows, setRows }

  return (
    <TableContext.Provider value={value}>
      <TableStyle>
        {rows.map(row => {
          <TableRow row={row} />
        })}
      </TableStyle>
    </TableContext.Provider>
  )
}
```

In the preceding code, the `Table` component is responsible for displaying all the rows of a table. The passed-in `rows` and `cols`, as well as a `setRows` dispatch function, are all sent to the `TableContext` provider to be consumed. With this, we can define a custom `DeleteCell` component:

```jsx
const DeleteCell = () => {
  const { row, rows, setRows } = useContext(TableContext)
  const onClick = () => {
    const newRows = rows.filter(r => r.title !== row.title)
    setRows(newRows)
  }

  return (
    <div>
      <button onClick={onClick}>Remove</button>
    </div>
  )
}
```

In the preceding code, `DeleteCell` contains a **Remove** button. When clicked, it first assembles the new table rows, `newRows`, by filtering out the current `row` and then uses the `setRows` dispatch function to replace the table content. Once `rows` is updated, it should trigger a provider update and thereby propagate a change to all table components.

Without a context to provide `setRows`, it would have to be passed through lots of layers to reach `DeleteCell`. Even in this brief example, the number of layers is not straightforward. Moreover, in this case, we don't exactly know the name of the component beforehand. It could be `DeleteCell` or `DefaultCell`, or any cell component that hasn't been designed yet. Therefore, the context usage here is really helpful in delivering things to an area underneath without knowing the exact location.

> **Playground – Table Context**
>
> Feel free to play with this online example at `https://codepen.io/windmaomao/pen/VwzWeMa`.

Let's conclude this table example by means of `Table` component usage under the `App` component:

```
const cols = [
  { name: 'combo', Cell: ComboCell },
  { name: 'action', Cell: DeleteCell }
]
const App = () => {
  const [rows, setRows] = useState(fruits)
  return <Table
    rows={rows}
    cols={cols}
    setRows={setRows}
  />
}
```

Summary

We learned a really cool concept in this chapter, that is, a context. First, we got to know what is a context under *React*. We then dug deeper into the context design as well as how to consume it with a `useContext` hook. We then went through a context test drive by managing a user object for a site and further learned two more applications of applying contexts to the `Theme` and the `Table`.

In the next chapter, we will get into our next hook in the *React* family and see how a ref can be used to hide private matters away from the engine.

Questions and answers

The following are some questions and answers to refresh your knowledge:

1. What is a *React* context?

    A *React* context is an identity that can be used to share a value with consumers. It's designed so that a value can be provided to a localized scope, hence all components within that scope can read from this shared value.

2. What is the useContext hook?

    The useContext hook is used in a consumer component so that it can read a context given by providers. A component can consume as many contexts as it can. When the provider gets updated, all the consumer components for that particular context get updated at the same time.

3. What's the common usage of useContext?

    The useContext hook is a hook in the *React* hook family when it comes to an update involving an area of components. We often see this context usage in User, Theme, and Table, which requires the consumption of a value under an ancestor component without passing it explicitly through layers of components. The useContext hook also makes it possible to deliver a value to an area without knowing exactly where the destination is.

Appendix

Appendix A – Propagating a context

React comes with different kinds of fibers. While a function component is one of them, the context provider is another one. It gets its own update logic with each update:

```
function updateContextProvider(fiber) {
  var providerType = fiber.type
  var context = providerType._context
  var newProps = fiber.pendingProps
  var oldProps = fiber.memoizedProps
  var newValue = newProps.value
  if (oldProps !== null) { ... }
  var children = newProps.children
  reconcileChildren(fiber, children)
  return fiber.child
}
```

In the preceding code, the `updateContextProvider` function takes in `fiber`, and checks whether it has been mounted or not via `oldProps !== null`. If it's a first-time mount, then it does things similar to a function component, reconciling the children into fibers and then returning the first child to work on next.

If it's not the first time, such as during an update, it then compares the `value` prop between `oldValue` and `newValue`:

```
if (oldProps !== null) {
  var oldValue = oldProps.value
  if (oldValue === newValue) {
    if (oldProps.children === newProps.children) {
      return bailoutOnAlreadyFinishedWork(fiber)
    }
  } else {
    propagateContextChange(fiber, context)
  }
}
```

If it turns out that there's no change in the value provided from the strict equal comparison, `===`, and if there's no change in the children, it then bails out the fiber and skips the reconciliation. Otherwise, if there's a change in the value provided, it propagates the context change to all its consumer fibers via the `propagateContextChange` function:

```
function propagateContextChange(work, context) {
  var fiber = work.child;
  while (fiber !== null) {
    var nextFiber = void 0
    var list = fiber.dependencies;
    if (list !== null) {
      nextFiber = fiber.child;
      var dependency = list.firstContext;
      while (dependency !== null) {
        if (dependency.context === context) {
          scheduleWorkOnParentPath(fiber.return)
          break
        }
        dependency = dependency.next;
      }
    } else {
      nextFiber = fiber.child;
    }
    ...
    fiber = nextFiber;
```

```
      }
   }
```

The propagation goes for a deep search under the `fiber` fiber and checks to see whether it contains the same `context` as per the `firstContext`. If it finds a match, it invokes a `scheduleWorkOnParentPath` function to schedule an update along the path from the root to the parent. This function is quite similar to `scheduleUpdateOnFiber`, which we see in the `useState` hook. But here, instead of doing it once, this function is applied to all consumers found.

In short, you can see that a provider is a special component that schedules an update for all consumers reading from the same context.

Appendix B – Context scope and value

A context value changes under different scopes of a context. But what does this statement mean?

```
Const provider1 = (value) => {
   const provider2 = (value) => {
      const provider3 = (value) => {
         console.log(value)
      }
      provider3(3)
   }
   provider2(2)
}
provider1(1)
```

In the preceding convoluted example, can you guess what the output is if we invoke `provider1(1)`? Please take a minute to think. The answer is 3.

Because each function has a scope, within the scope of the function, all local variables from the input argument take precedence. Though the outer `value` is 1, the inner `value` becomes 3 due to the change of scope.

The context provider is designed in a similar fashion; it uses a stack to push the old value in before entering one scope, and then pop the old value out after leaving the same scope. This way, an outer scope is always kept in memory when we work in an inner scope.

Let's take a look at this process closely. Say `cursor` holds the value in one outer scope, and it wants to enter the inner scope with a new `value`:

```
function push(cursor, value) {
  index++
  valuesStack[index] = cursor.current
  cursor.current = value
}
```

In the preceding code, `cursor` is a global variable, which holds the current value under the `current` property. The `push` operation puts the old value in the stack and then replaces the current value of `cursor` with the new `value`.

Therefore, once we enter the inner scope, the `current` of `cursor` is updated to the latest, so how do we get back the old value once we finish this inner scope? Yes, we perform a pop operation:

```
function pop(cursor) {
  if (index < 0) return
  cursor.current = valueStack[index]
  valueStack[index] = null
  index--
}
```

In the preceding code, we pop the previous stacked value back to the `cursor`. So now, when we get out of the inner scope, the value gets back to the old value.

This mechanism is exactly what's applied to our context provider:

```
function updateContextProvider(fiber) {
  ...
  pushProvider(fiber, newValue)
  if (oldProps !== null) { ... }
  ...
}
```

When it gets to the update of a provider, it pushes the old value and replaces it with a new value with a `pushProvider` function:

```
function pushProvider(fiber, nextValue) {
  var context = fiber.type._context
  push(valueCursor, context._currentValue)
  context._currentValue = nextValue;
}
```

The last line of pushProvider sets the _currentValue of the context with the nextValue from the value prop. This is how the consumer in the inner scope gets the inner value. But before that, it pushes an old value of _currentValue in the stack and stores it in a global variable, valueCursor.

Before we move out of the provider's scope, popProvider is invoked:

```
function popProvider(fiber) {
  var currentValue = valueCursor.current
  pop(valueCursor)
  var context = fiber.type._context
  context._currentValue = currentValue
}
```

The last line of popProvider sets the currentValue of the context back to the saved value from valueCursor. But before that, it pops the old value from the stack.

So, at all times, there's a valueCursor to hold the outer scope value, while context._currentValue holds the current/inner scope value. This means that the context value stored in _currentValue is not a fixed value throughout the update. Hopefully, you can now see that a context has a "global" sense and varies based on the scope.

8

Use Ref to Hide Stuff

In the previous chapter, we learned how the *React* context is designed and how to use a useContext hook to make an update for an area. In this chapter, we will introduce another *React* entity, a ref. We will learn how to access a *DOM* element via a ref and walk through the design and source code behind the useRef hook. We will also describe how to work with a persistent value without dispatching an update. In the end, we'll apply refs to a couple of practical problems, such as clicking outside of the menu, avoiding memory leaks, setting up a mule, and locating the current value. And we'll also reveal two bonus topics in the *Appendix* section, the callback ref and forward ref.

We will cover the following topics in this chapter:

- Accessing *DOM* elements
- Understanding useRef design
- State without an update
- Test driving useRef
- useRef examples
- Questions and answers
- Appendix

Accessing DOM elements

Before a modern *UI* framework is introduced, to make a change to the screen, we work directly with a *DOM* element:

```
<body>
  <h1 id="title"></h1>
</body>
<script>
  const el = document.getElementById('#title')
  el.textContent = "Hello World"
</script>
```

The preceding *HTML* file defines an h1 element tagged with a specific id value. So we can use the id value to find the el element and make a change to its textContent. This is how a *DOM* element gets updated:

Hello World

Figure 8.1 – HTML displaying the Hello World title

With React, we can achieve the preceding functionality by wrapping elements in a component, such as a function component:

```
const Title = () => {
  const [title, setTitle] = useState("")
  useEffect(() => { setTitle("Hello World") }, [])
  return <h1>{title}</h1>
}
```

The benefits of using the preceding functional approach are that it provides an abstraction on top of the physical *DOM* and allows us to focus our development in a localized space. This way, we can safely put our logic and design without worrying that other code might accidentally touch this space. It makes our development more productive.

This is a good thing, and here's a question. Can we still get hold of the *DOM* element using id as it used to be? Because the job of *React* isn't to reinvent all *DOM* functionalities, and sometimes we do need to work with the elements directly:

```
const Title = () => {
  return <h1 id="title">{title}</h1>
}
```

In the preceding code, we add `id` to the `h1` element. But we run into some problems quickly. First, the `Title` component is made to be reused. This means we can have multiple `<Title />` instances on the current screen. Suppose we want to operate on one of them – how do know which instance to find by using `id`?

Secondly, and more importantly, say we find the element we want. Since it's wrapped in a component now, *React* manages its life cycle, so how do we know the moment when it gets mounted and unmounted precisely? If we're not sure about this, how can we safely operate on it?

Both problems are tricky but need to be addressed before we can directly work with an element under a component. Let's see how *React* solves them.

Attach and de-attach

So, when exactly does the element in a component mount and unmount? To answer this question, we need to first look at the element returned from a component closely:

```
return <h1>{title}</h1>
```

What does the preceding statement return? Is it a *DOM* element, as we put in the *HTML* file? Though it looks quite like one, the compiler says otherwise:

```
return createElement('h1', null, title)
```

Actually, what the compiler sees is a *JavaScript* statement with a `createElement` function returning a *React* element. It takes three input arguments, the element type (`h1`), the props (`null`), and the children (`title`), and the returned element is commonly referred to as a virtual *DOM*. If you are interested in learning more about `createElement` usage, check out the *Adopting CSS-in-JS approach* section of *Chapter 10, Building a Website with React*.

When the first update starts, *React* takes this element, reconciles it into a fiber, and appends it to the tree. It then moves on to its children. For all child elements, it reconciles them and appends them as children fibers. This continues until all elements are reconciled into the tree.

After all the fibers are prepared, *React* performs a one-time commit to create all *DOM* elements on the screen. So, essentially, the physical *DOM* elements aren't created until the full tree is updated in memory. So, only by then, *React* hands us the element instance if we ask for it:

```
return <h1 ref={ref}>Hello World</h1>
```

In the preceding code, a `ref` object is passed to the `h1` element as a prop and it behaves as a storage container, asking *React* to store the element instance once available. This `ref` container takes a specific format:

```
ref = { current: null }
```

After the instance of the *DOM* element is created, the preceding `ref` is populated in the `commitAttachRef` function during the **Commit** phase:

```
function commitAttachRef(fiber, instance) {
  const ref = fiber.ref
  if (ref !== null) {
    ref.current = instance
  }
}
```

In the preceding `commitAttachRef` function, when `ref` is provided and initialized, its `current` property gets assigned from the *DOM* instance. This is for the mount. Similarly, when the *DOM* element is about to be removed, `current` gets assigned back to `null` in the `commitDetachRef` function during the **Commit** phase:

```
function commitDetachRef(fiber) {
  var ref = fiber.ref
  if (ref !== null) {
    ref.current = null
  }
}
```

With this capability, as long as we provide `ref` to an element, React assigns the element's instance into `ref.current` upon the mount and unmount. We can use `ref.current` to work on the element as it used to be. This is the *React* way of accessing *DOM* elements.

There's a subtlety here. Note that when passing the element's instance over when it's ready, the assignment is done with `ref.current = instance` instead of `ref = instance`. This is because *React* designs `ref` as a container to be available during the life cycle of the component. Put simply, the container is always valid, whereas the value under the `current` property can change along the way.

The `ref` prop we used so far is a ref in an object format, which is the most popular and easy-to-use format. Other than this, *React* supports one more format in other situations. If you are interested, you can check out *Appendix A – Callback ref* at the end of this chapter.

Now we know what a *React* ref is, let's take a look at how to create one under a function component with a `useRef` hook.

Understanding useRef design

React provides a useRef hook to create a ref:

```
const Title = () => {
  const ref = useRef(null)
  return <h1 ref={ref}>Hello World</h1>
}
```

The useRef hook takes an initial value as its only input argument and returns a ref object, putting that initial value under the current property.

There's no additional data structure required for useRef, other than the basic fiber hook support:

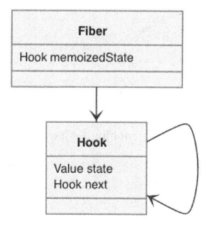

Figure 8.2 – useRef design

Just like useState and useEffect uses state to store state and the effect, useRef uses state to store the ref. Next, let's take a look at how it's implemented.

The useRef hook follows a typical hook setup where it takes a path of either mountRef or updateRef, depending on whether the fiber is under mount or update via the isFiberMounting flag, as explained in *Chapter 3, Hooking into React*:

```
function useRef(initialValue) {
  if (isFiberMounting) {
    return mountRef(initialValue)
  } else {
    return updateRef()
  }
}
```

When under mount, it first gets the hook by creating one:

```
function mountRef(initialValue) {
  const hook = mountHook()
  const ref = { current: initialValue }
  hook.state = ref
  return ref
}
```

Before returning the `ref` object, the initial value is stored under the `current` property and `ref` is stored under `state` of the hook.

After the component is mounted, the next time it gets updated and arrives at the `useRef` hook, it gets the hook by cloning one:

```
function updateRef() {
  const hook = updateHook()
  return hook.state
}
```

Once we have the hook, we can get `ref` from `state` and return it. Also, note that the hook doesn't accept any input argument after the mount.

By far, this is the shortest hook implementation we have seen. The following diagram shows the workflow:

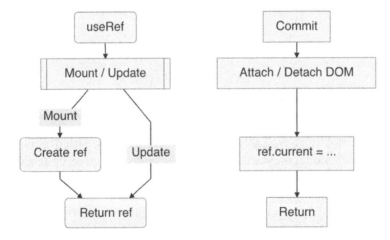

Figure 8.3 – useRef workflow

In short, the `useRef` hook provides the basic storage for persisting a ref. A `ref` stored in the hook never gets updated after the mount where the `current` value is initialized. Basically, the `useRef` hook essentially lets us manage the state out of the box.

If ref is wired as a prop to an element, when the element gets mounted or unmounted, its *DOM* instance gets updated in the current property.

Now we know the design of the useRef hook. If the ref created is used to hold a value, how is it different from the useState hook? Since they both can hold a value, let's spend some time comparing them to understand more about the useRef hook.

State without an update

The ref created via useRef can be used to hold not only a DOM instance but also any value. At any time, we can change its current property with a new assignment:

```
ref.current = ...
```

The assignment can be a *JavaScript* expression. What's special about this is that *the ref assignment doesn't do anything more than an assignment*. This implies that it does not trigger an update. Let's take a look at how it impacts the UI when we wire it to a user action:

```
const Title = () => {
  const ref = useRef(null)
  const onClick = () => {
    ref.current = 'white'
  }
  return <Child color={ref} onClick={onClick} />
}
```

In the preceding code, an event handler is wired with the Child component, and when the user clicks, it assigns a color into ref.current. It looks pretty similar to the case using a useState hook. If we were using a useState hook, the code would look like the following:

```
const Title = () => {
  const [color, setColor] = useState('')
  const onClick = () => {
    setColor('white')
  }
  return <Child color={color} onClick={onClick} />
}
```

When comparing these two cases, we can see that the main difference is the following line:

```
// ref version
ref.current = 'white'
// state version
setColor('white')
```

In the ref case, it is a plain assignment, whereas in the state case, it dispatches an update to schedule the state change. This means that the state case is a lot more complicated than the ref case. We can even simulate the ref case with a state:

```
const Title = () => {
  const [obj] = useState({ color: '' })
  const onClick = () => {
    obj.color = 'white'
  }
  return <Child color={obj} onClick={onClick} />
}
```

In the preceding experiment, we made the state an obj with a color property. And this obj is quite comparable to ref from useRef, because obj.color = is also a plain assignment:

```
obj.color = 'white'
```

You might wonder, for plain assignments, what happens to the color prop wired with either ref or obj? Interestingly, in both cases, nothing happens. Because with a plain assignment, there's no dispatch to the Title component, thus there isn't any update to the Child component. Therefore, even though the content gets changed, *React* wouldn't respond to that.

So, essentially, a ref can be taken to hold a value without the update capability. This also explains why the source code of useRef is so compact, because it doesn't do much other than returning a persistent value.

Now that we've gone over the design of a ref and the useRef hook, let's take it for a test drive.

Test driving useRef

There's always a chance that *React* runs short in terms of controlling the internals of a *DOM* element. Say there's an input and a button, as in *Figure 8.4*. Upon a button click, we want to manually focus on the input:

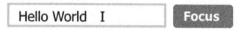

Figure 8.4 – Focus input

Normally, if we click the button, it gets focused, and if we click somewhere else, it loses focus. But in this case, after we click the **Focus** button, we want to focus the input instead of the button so that the user can type right away.

Let's see how we can apply `useRef` to make this happen:

```
const Title = () => {
  const ref = useRef()
  const onClick = () => {
    ref.current.focus()
  }

  return (
    <>
      <input ref={ref} />
      <button onClick={onClick}>focus</button>
    </>
  )
}
```

In the preceding example, after `input` is mounted, its instance is stored in `ref.current`. When we click the button, the event handler uses the ref to invoke a native *DOM* `focus` method to make the input focused. That's it!

Though the `ref` object is always valid, the `current` property is not necessarily valid all the time. Before the mount finishes, it can store a `null` value. After the unmount, it can store a `null` value as well. So, to make sure that we don't run into any runtime error, we normally add a check before using it:

```
if (ref.current) ref.current.focus()
```

Sometimes, you see the following short-circuit way:

```
ref.current && ref.current.focus()
```

It's important to note that, although we get to use `ref` to control the *DOM* element, React wouldn't know the impact of your code. For instance, in our example, *React* can't tell whether the input gets focused or not. In order for React to know that, we still need to add a state to keep track of this change:

```
const Title = () => {
  const [focused, setFocused] = useState(false)
  const ref = useRef()
  const onClick = () => {
    ref.current.focus()
    setFocused(true)
  }

  ...
}
```

In a way, getting hold of the raw DOM elements gives us the extra capability to manipulate the element behind React's back.

> **Playground – Focusing Input**
>
> Feel free to play with this online example at `https://codepen.io/windmaomao/pen/WNZwoje`

Controlling a child ref

Since a ref is basically an object, it can be passed around as a prop to a child component. Therefore, a passed-in `ref` object can be attached to a DOM element inside a child:

```
const Child = ({ childRef }) => {
  return <input ref={childRef} />
}
```

Utilizing this `childRef`, the `Child` component allows the parent to operate on it:

```
const Title = () => {
  const ref = useRef()
  const onClick = () => {
    ref.current.focus()
  }
  return (
    <>
      <Child childRef={ref} />
      <button onClick={onClick}>focus</button>
    </>
```

```
  )
}
```

In the preceding code, the `Title` component creates a `ref` object via `useRef` and passes it to `Child` via a `childRef` prop. When `Child` mounts, it populates the `input` instance into `ref.current`. And when we click on the button, it invokes the `focus` method of the input element of `Child`. This allows a parent component to control a *DOM* element of `Child`.

Note that the prop we used is named `childRef` instead of `ref` because `ref` is a reserved prop name to attach a *DOM* instance, whereas `childRef` is merely a regular prop to pass in an object. Although both are props, the `ref` prop is a special one. It would be wrong if we mistakenly used `ref` instead of `childRef` in this example:

```
<Child ref={ref} />
```

The preceding line would ask the `Child` function component to assign its instance to `ref`. But a function component cannot have a ref by default. Therefore, avoid using the ref name when passing it around. There's actually a way to attach a ref to a function component with some work; if you are interested, you can find out more in the *Appendix B – Forward ref* section at the end of this chapter.

Now that we have used a ref to control the element in the component, let's take a look at more examples of using `useRef`.

useRef examples

A ref is powerful. Because *React* makes things very reactive, if we want to either disable this reactiveness or add a tweak to it, the ref gives us the opportunity to do that. In this section, we'll look into more examples of how it can be used to solve interesting problems in *React*.

Clicking outside the menu

Say you have a component, and you want to know when the user clicks outside of it. This is a very popular feature for a popup menu or a modal. Once the menu is visible, we want to dismiss it when the user clicks anywhere outside of it:

Figure 8.5 – Click outside to dismiss

Let's say we have a `Menu` component displaying a list of menu items:

```
const Menu = () => {
  const [on, setOOn] = useState(true)
  if (!on) return null
  return (
    <ul>
      <li>Home</li>
      <li>Price</li>
      <li>Produce</li>
      <li>Support</li>
      <li>About</li>
    </ul>
  )
}
```

In the preceding code, an `on` state is created and set to `true` initially, thus making a list of the menu items visible. But when we click outside of this list, we'd want to set `on` to `false` to hide it. For simplicity, here we define the `on` flag inside the `Menu` component, but in practice, it could be passed from the parent as a prop.

We know how to find out when the user clicks the `Menu` component using an event handler, but how do we know when the user clicks somewhere outside? Do we need to know the location of all the components on the entire screen?

This is the place we can attach a `ref` to the `ul` element:

```
const Menu = () => {
  const [on, setOn] = useState(true)
  const ref = useRef()
  if (!on) return null
  return (
    <ul ref={ref}>
      ...
    </ul>
  )
}
```

Instead of attaching the click event handler to one element, we can listen to a `mousedown` window event. This way, we are aware of any user click, regardless of whether it's inside or outside the `Menu` component:

```
const Menu = () => {
  const ref = useRef()
  useEffect(() => {
    const listener = e => { ... }
    window.addEventListener('mousedown', listener)
    return () => {
      window.removeEventListener('mousedown', listener)
    }
  }, [])
  ...
}
```

In the preceding code, we registered an event handler for a `mousedown` window event, so with any mouse click, it'll invoke our `listener` function. Upon the unmount, we also make sure that we remove this event handler via a `destroy` function.

When the `mousedown` handler is fired, we can use `ref` to find out whether the mouse location is contained inside the boundary of the `ul` element:

```
const listener = e => {
  if (!ref.current) return
  if (!ref.current.contains(e.target)) {
    setOn(false)
  }
}
```

In the preceding `listener` handler, upon each `mousedown` event, we check whether the element has been mounted via `ref.current`, and then we check whether the element under the mouse, via `e.target`, is a child of the `ul` element. If the user clicks any children inside the `ul`, then we know they have clicked inside. And if not, we know the user has clicked outside, and then we can dispatch to set the `on` state to be `false`, thus dismissing the display of the menu.

Playground – Click Outside of Menu

Feel free to play with this online example at `https://codepen.io/windmaomao/pen/XWaerGm`.

In short, with the help of the ref, we can invoke `contains` functions to find out whether an element is inside another element.

Avoiding memory leaks

Historically speaking, a ref was created to hold a DOM element, but people later found it very effective in addressing tricky problems. One problem is memory leaks, which happen when performing an async action. The thing about an async operation is that the callback function gets invoked later. By the time the callback is handled, there's a chance the component (or any variable associated with the component) is not valid anymore.

Let's say we fetch an API and display the result as `text`:

```
const Title = () => {
  const [text, setText] = useState("")
  useEffect(() => {
    fetch("https://google.com").then(res => {
      setText(res.title)
    })
  }, [])
  return <h1>{text}</h1>
}
```

The preceding code is a common fetch process, but there's a memory leak lurking out there. When it happens, the browser outputs the following message:

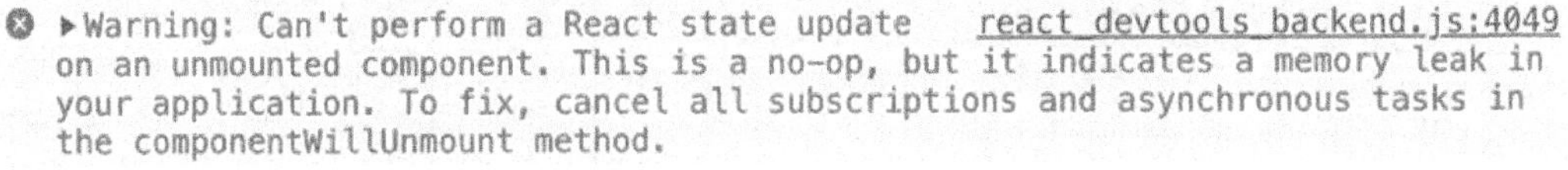

❌ ▶Warning: Can't perform a React state update   react_devtools_backend.js:4049
  on an unmounted component. This is a no-op, but it indicates a memory leak in
  your application. To fix, cancel all subscriptions and asynchronous tasks in
  the componentWillUnmount method.

Figure 8.6 – Memory leak warning message

Although *React* is nice enough to display it as a warning message under development build, it's actually an error, as it says **indicates a memory leak** in the message. The strange thing about this leak is that most of time, the *UI* continues to function even after the message. So, shall we ignore this message? Absolutely not.

Let's build the crime scene and try to understand what exactly happens under this message:

```
const App = ({ flag }) => {
  if (flag) return <Title />
  return null
}
```

Say you have an App parent component that displays Title based on a flag. For one update, the flag becomes false, thus Title gets unmounted and the screen turns blank. This is valid business logic, so why is it a problem?

The problem lies inside the Title component instead of App. Precisely, when Title mounts, the *API* fetch starts, but the fetch might not finish soon enough before the unmount. The flag and the fetch are two independent things. Therefore, Title can have unfinished business after the unmount. Say the time arrives to handle the unfinished business, such as the callback function – what happens to the setText statement? Should it raise another update when the component has gone?

Technically, if the component is unmounted, it can't be updated anymore. Moreover, every hook is registered under the fiber, and if the fiber has been removed, then nothing registered under it should be accessed anymore. Otherwise, inconsistency would emerge, such as a memory leak.

So back to our case, when an async call returns after the unmount – this becomes a solid bug that we can't just ignore. This bug happens quite often in situations when a conditional statement makes the code to switch to another branch of update, such as a route switch. Most of the memory leaks are difficult to debug, so we should try to avoid them at all costs.

Playground – Memory Leak

Feel free to play with this online example at `https://codepen.io/windmaomao/pen/VwzMYNL`.

In order to see the memory leak message, you need to open the **Browser developer** panel and switch to the **Console** tab.

To resolve this bug, what we need to do is to carefully guard the content of the callback function, based on whether the `Title` component is still mounted or not:

```
const Title = () => {
  const [text, setText] = useState("")
  const mountedRef = useRef(true)
  useEffect(() => {
    fetch("https://google.com").then(res => {
      if (!mountedRef.current) return
      setText(res.title)
    })
    return () => {
      mountedRef.current = false
    }
  }, [])
}
```

In the preceding code, we add `mountedRef` to indicate whether `Title` is mounted or not. We initially set it to `true`, because when the component gets updated, we assume it's safe to dispatch more updates. And after the unmount via `useEffect`, we set the `mountedRef` flag to be `false` in the `destroy` function.

Now, in the callback handler of the fetch, we check if it's still mounted by reading `mountedRef`. And if it's `false`, we cancel the handler operation without moving forward to access any internal method, such as `setText`. This means even when the *API* is successful, there's no update to bring this value to the screen anymore.

> **Playground – Avoid Memory Leaks**
>
> Feel free to play with this online example at `https://codepen.io/windmaomao/pen/wvqraKP`.

You might wonder why we can't use a state instead of a ref for the `mountRef` purpose. Let's say we replace `mountRef` with a `mounted` state:

```
const Title = () => {
  const [mounted, setMounted] = useState(true)
  useEffect(() => {
    ...
    return () => {
      setMounted(false)
    }
  }, [])
}
```

Although creative, the preceding code wouldn't work. Because, essentially, you ask to dispatch a new update after the unmount, it's the exact memory leak we want to avoid. In *Chapter 5, Use Effect to Handle Side Effects*, we learned that the `destroy` function of a passive effect is last called after all DOM elements settle, so by then, we shouldn't be allowed to access any internal method.

This example also tells us that a change from a ref is not meant to be reflected in the UI, whereas a state is designed to be in sync with the UI at all times.

Setting up a mule

When we design a web application, we tend not to have a global variable, because we know it's so easy that their usage can lead to some unmanageable side effects. On the other hand, if we have some global information that is valid for the entire site, it's still handy if we want to share it with the rest of the app behind the scenes. So, what kind of compromise can we have in this situation?

In *Chapter 7, Use Context to Cover an Area*, we learned to create a context to share info for a site. We can provide the info at the very top of the tree, the `App` component:

```
const App = () => {
  const [value, setValue] = useState(0)
  return (
    <AppContext.Provider value={{ value, setValue }}>
      ...
    </AppContext.Provider>
  )
}
```

A fact of using the state in the preceding code is that, when changing a value through the `setValue` dispatch function, it causes the whole site to update, which can be a very expensive operation. If we don't need to notify the user of this change, we can use a ref instead:

```
const App = () => {
  const value = useRef({
    count: 1
  })
  const onIncrement = () => {
value.current.count++
  }
  return (
    <AppContext.Provider value={value}>
      <button onClick={onIncrement}>+<button>
      <Title />
```

```
        </AppContext.Provider>
    )
}
```

In the preceding code, a ref is created with `useRef` to hold a custom `count` value under the `current` property. We can increment it as used to be with a button click via `onIncrement`. We also add a `Title` component underneath to consume this `count` value:

```
const Title = () => {
  const { current } = useContext(AppContext)
  return <div>{current.count}</div>
}
```

In the preceding `Title` component, it consumes `current` from `AppContext`, and displays the stored `count` value. With this setup, if you click `onIncrement` in the `App` component, the `number` value always stays at `0`. It seems our `count` is broken.

To reveal what's happened, let's add a manual update to the `Title` component with a button:

```
const Title = () => {
  const { current } = useContext(AppContext)
  const [number, setNumber] = useState(current.count)
  const onClick = () => {
    setNumber(current.count)
  }
  return <button onClick={onClick}>{number}</button>
}
```

In the preceding code, we put the `count` value into a local `number` state, so we can use `setNumber` to make an update. Now, upon clicking `number` via `onClick`, you will see the latest `current.count` value on the screen, as shown in *Figure 8.7*:

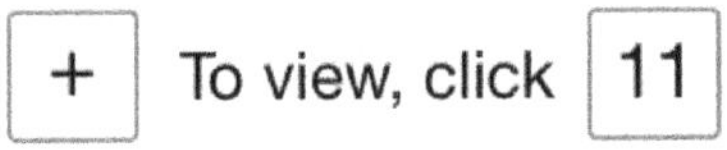

Figure 8.7 – A count state with a separate update

It's a bit intriguing here to see the process of how the number got displayed on the screen. First, we incremented it, and then we revealed it. Therefore, `current.count` isn't broken; it's just not in sync with the screen.

> **Playground – Mule Context**
>
> Feel free to play with this online example at `https://codepen.io/windmaomao/pen/YzxrXQN`.

With a context like `AppContext`, we can store the value and use it freely decoupled from the display. In a way, the ref context becomes a mule that can move any data (or functionalities) from one component to another one under *React*'s nose. Practically, this kind of context is an effective approach when you need to bring in a third-party library that does not necessarily wire with *React* that tightly but that you want to be operational along with *React*.

Locating the current value

The `current` property being current is the unique thing about a ref. The property name *current* under the ref is given for a reason because, technically, there's nothing more current than a ref in React.

When we use a `useState` hook, we want to find out the current updated value of a state. Although we use the same word, current, the state can't be that current in some situations. We will use an example to demonstrate that.

Let's say we have a button to increment a count, but instead of incrementing it right away, it waits for 3 seconds after the click:

```
function Title() {
  const [count, setCount] = useState(0)
  const onClick = () => {
    setTimeout(() => {
      console.log('clicked', count) ①
      setCount(count + 1)
    }, 3000)
  }
  console.log('updated', count)       ②
  return <button onClick={onClick}>+</button>
}
```

In the preceding code, `setTimeout` is used in the event handler to deliberately delay the `setCount` function by 3 seconds. What we expect to see is that each click should behave like a delayed click where the `count` value increments to 1, 2, and 3 on the screen 3 seconds later.

When we run the code, it shows differently, as shown in the next timeline:

```
|--------------0-0--0----> clicked   ①
0--------------1-1--1---> updated     ②
```

After we clicked the buttons three times in a row and waited for 3 seconds, we didn't see `count` incremented to 3 on screen. Instead, we saw it incremented to 1. Quite surprising?

> **Playground – Where is the Current Value?**
>
> Feel free to play with this online example at `https://codepen.io/windmaomao/pen/ZEJXbEG`.

How could three dispatches end up with one dispatch? Let's debug by adding two more series to the timeline, the `"x"` click and the `"R"` update:

```
        0.5s      3.5s
|-----x-x--x-------------> click
|--------------0-0--0----> clicked   ①
R--------------R-R------> update
0--------------1-1------> updated     ②
```

When we clicked the button for the first time (at about `t=0.5s`), what was the `count` value from the event handler? It was 0, our initial state. Then, when we clicked the button the second time, what was the `count` value from the event handler? You would say, it's got to be 1, right, since I clicked it? But unfortunately, it wasn't the case.

Looking at the `"updated"` series, the second update didn't arrive right away after the click. If there was no new update, `count` continued to hold an old state. Since the new update didn't arrive until three seconds later (at about `t=3.5s`), during this period, any event handler would still carry the same `count`. Okay, that explains why the `"clicked"` series printed 0 upon each click. It was almost like all the three clicks performed the same dispatch statement:

```
const onClick = () => {
  setTimeout(() => {
    setCount(0 + 1)          // count = 0
  }, 3000)
}
```

Essentially, we dispatched to request a change to 1 three times. In our case, all clicks happened before the second update. This created an out-of-sync moment. This is not a design flaw, since `count` is only designed for pointing to a copy in the current update. Unless it's made of a pointer pointing to the same memory space, it can't be pointing to the current value.

A common misconception is to refer to `setState` as an assignment. By now, you should see that it's incorrect, since it actually requests an assignment instead of executing the assignment. The request takes time to be handled and executed, and moreover, the assignment can be revoked due to optimization. The fate of this assignment from `setState` isn't crystal clear, whereas in the ref case, the assignment is plain, instant, and can't be missed.

Let's apply a ref to fix this problem:

```
function Title() {
  const [count, setCount] = useState(0)
  const ref = useRef(0)
  const onClick = () => {
    setTimeout(() => {
      ref.current++
      setCount(ref.current)
      console.log('clicked', ref.current) ①
    }, 3000)
  }
  console.log('updated', count)        ②
  ...
}
```

We can confirm this via the following timeline sketch:

```
|-----0.5s-----3.5s------> time
|-----x-x--x-------------> click
|---------------1-2--3----> clicked  ①
R--------------R-R--R---> update
0--------------1-2--3---> updated  ②
```

Okay, now everything works after we used a ref to store the number along with the `count` state. The `ref.count++` statement increments the current number and continues to store the updated number. Here, we used both a state and a ref to keep track of a single number. It's overkill, and we do it here to merely demonstrate the solution. In the *useCurrent hook* section of *Chapter 9, Use Custom Hooks to Reuse Logic*, we will refine this approach into something more practical.

> **Playground – Locate the Current Value**
>
> Feel free to play with this online example at `https://codepen.io/windmaomao/pen/eYEGpJJ`.

There's a simpler solution to this problem and it doesn't involve a ref. Remember, a `useState` hook supports another functional format:

```
const onClick = () => {
  setTimeout(() => {
    setCount(v => v + 1)
  }, 3000)
}
```

In the preceding code, a functional format setter is used so that we can read out the current state through v, because we want to know exactly what the current state is before committing it. The `v => v + 1` statement becomes essential, and sometimes we can even put some logic inside this function:

```
setCount(v => {
  // perform some action
  // based on the current v
  return v
})
```

It doesn't seem like the preceding location is the right place to perform other business logic than the value update; however, based on the `useState` design, this actually is the only supported location where you can read the current state consistently. We even returned the current v value back, which implies that we only want to get the current value but are not interested in a new update. You can take this as a made-up `getCount` access function for a state.

All in all, both solutions reveal the fact that in the current update, the state value can get out of sync with its underlying current value.

You might have a question at this point – if a ref is that powerful and flexible, why don't we just use it to replace the state? The answer to this question lies in the dilemma that the state that *React* wants developers to use is a managed state that takes care of the dispatch upon any state change. However, a ref is a raw state with which the developers still have to manage every other aspect of the *UI* update. In a way, if we were using refs for everything, then we would not need to use *React* at all because the point of a ref is to hide stuff without catching the engine's attention.

Summary

In this chapter, we first learned what a *React* ref is. We then went over how to access a *DOM* element by using a ref and went through the design of the `useRef` hook, and saw how to persist a value without triggering a *UI* update. We also gave `useRef` a test drive by walking through an input focus example. In the end, we went through how special it is by showing more examples of its use, including clicking outside of a menu, avoiding memory leaks, setting up a mule, and locating the current value.

In the next chapter, we will put all the hooks we have learned so far together and see how to finally create your custom hook, tailored to solve your own problems.

Questions and answers

Here are some questions and answers to refresh your knowledge:

1. What is a ref?

    A *React* ref is a container to hold a persistent value. In general, you can use the value as a raw state with no update capability.

2. What is `useRef`?

    A `useRef` hook can be used to create a ref in a function component. Once created, it can be used as a persistent container during the life cycle of the component.

3. What are the common usages of `useRef`?

    One major usage of `useRef` is to hold a *DOM* instance that can be used to invoke native *DOM* functionalities. Another major usage of `useRef` is to sneak behind React to do something without kicking off the engine accidentally.

Appendix

Appendix A – Callback ref

React comes with two ways of receiving an element instance via the `ref` prop. The easiest one is the one we introduced, the object format. But there's another one called a callback ref that takes a functional format:

```
function commitAttachRef(fiber, instance) {
  var ref = fiber.ref;

  if (ref !== null) {
    if (typeof ref === 'function') {
```

```
      ref(instance)
    } else {
      ref.current = instance
    }
  }
}
```

Similarly, this functional format is supported when the *DOM* element is unmounted:

```
function commitDetachRef(fiber) {
  var ref = fiber.ref
  if (ref !== null) {
    if (typeof ref === 'function') {
      ref(null)
    } else {
      ref.current = null
    }
  }
}
```

During the DOM attachment or de-attachment, if it finds out the `ref` prop is provided as a functional format, it invokes it and passes the instance to it. Here's the usage:

```
const Title = () => {
  const ref = useRef()
  const onRef = (instance) => {
    ref.current = instance
  }
  return <h1 ref={onRef}>...</h1>
}
```

In the preceding code, an `onRef` function is wired to the `ref` prop. Both ways of setting the ref, either object or callback, are comparable. And the functional way seems to involve more work. So how is this functional format any more useful?

Although the `ref` object gives us the assigned *DOM* element, it doesn't tell us exactly when the *DOM* element is attached or de-attached. So, to capture these moments, we can use a ref callback:

```
const ref = useRef()
const setRef = (r) => {
  if (...) {
    ref.current = r
  } else {
    ...
  }
}
```

```
    }
    return <h1 ref={setRef}>...</h1>
```

In the preceding code, based on a condition, we could decide where we want to store this ref or which ref we want to store. The example only gives a very naïve implementation, but you can see that this provides us more room for custom logic in terms of managing the DOM instance.

Appendix B – Forward ref

A ref is created to store an instance of a class, whether the class is a *DOM* element or a class component. But not all components are written using a class, such as a function component:

```
function Title = () {
  return ...
}
// Not valid declaration
const ATitle = new Title()
// Not valid operation
ATitle.doSomething()
```

In the preceding code, we have declared `Title` as a function component. But since it's not declared with a class, we do not use `new` to create an instance. Instead, we invoke it via `Title()` at the update. Similarly, because of that, there's no way we can access the internal variables with an instance method such as `ATitle.dosomething()`.

This is why we mentioned earlier that we can't attach a ref to a function component; by default, it's not what a function component can provide:

```
    return <Title ref={ref} />
```

However, from a practical point of view, it does make sense for the developer to get hold of the `Title` instance and perform some action toward it. So, to address this need and to apply the ref idea consistently to all components, React provides one option called the forward ref:

```
const Title = React.forwardRef((props, ref) => {
  return (
    <h1 ref={ref}>
      {props.children}
    </h1>
  )
})
```

In the preceding setup, by using a `fowardRef` function provided by *React*, we can promote `ref` defined for an `h1` element as the ref of the `Title` component. What does this mean? Let's take a look at one usage:

```
const App = () => {
  const ref = useRef()
  const onClick = () => {
    ref.current.textContent = "Hello"
  }
  return <Title ref={ref} />
}
```

In the preceding `App` component, we can now treat `Title` similar to an `h1` element; when we change its content, it literally changes the `h1` text content inside `Title`. Essentially, a ref is passed from the child to the parent.

A function component, unlike a class component, does not have an instance method in *React*, so even when we have a ref now, we need to set up a custom method if we want to support one:

```
const Title = React.forwardRef((props, ref) => {
  useImperativeHandler(ref, () => ({
    go: () => { ref.current.focus() }
  }))
  return (
    <h1 ref={ref}>
      {props.children}
    </h1>
  )
})
```

In the preceding code, React provides a built-in hook called `useImperativeHandle` to allow us to customize the instance value. In this example, we add a go custom method for ref:

```
const App = () => {
  const ref = useRef()
  const onClick = () => {
    ref.current.go()
  }
  return <Title ref={ref} />
}
```

This way, when we ask the `Title` instance to go, it focuses on the `h1` element.

So, with `forwardRef` and `useImperativeHandle`, we add a ref to a function component. This provides more opportunity for the developer to add manual control to the function component. However, we need to understand that a ref passed from the child to the parent originates from a single element, so technically speaking, a ref done this way is still a ref of that element, not a real ref for the function component.

9

Use Custom Hooks to Reuse Logic

In the previous chapter, we learned how the `useRef` hook is designed and how to use a ref for a state without updating the screen. In this chapter, we will gather all the hooks we have learned about so far and see how to create a custom hook for our own needs. We will introduce what a custom hook is and then write some custom hooks step by step, including `useToggle`, `useWindow`, `useAsync`, `useDebounced`, `useClickOutside`, `useCurrent`, and `useProxy`.

We will cover the following topics in this chapter:

- Reviewing React hooks
- `useToggle`
- `useWindow`
- `useAsync`
- `useDebounced`
- `useClickOutside`
- `useCurrent`
- `useProxy`
- Questions and answers

Reviewing React hooks

We have seen quite a few hooks provided by *React*. Let's take a moment to review what we have learned so far:

- Update a state with the `useState` hook.

- Handle a side effect with the `useEffect` hook.

- Reuse the last value with the `useMemo` hook.

- Update an area with the `useContext` hook.

- Hide stuff from display with the `useRef` hook.

The `useState` hook is the most popular one, which is used to define a state and make it dispatchable to trigger a *UI* update. *React* wants us to use this as the main mechanism to be in sync with the screen. A mental picture of using it is that, as long as the state changes, the *UI* should produce an outcome accordingly. Otherwise, the *UI* should stay intact. Essentially, what that is saying is to make something happen on the screen, design a state and wire it with elements. This is the *React* way. If you take this as a baseline, it can help you understand anything else.

The `useEffect` hook allows us to listen to state changes, and based on that, we can perform an action such as a side effect. Therefore, with it, you are equipped with two ways to make something happen on the screen, that is, either listen to an event or a state change. The subtlety here is that the side effect doesn't get applied until all the *DOM* elements settle after the update. Also, don't forget to clean up the side effect, if any.

The `useMemo` hook serves as an optimization so that we can use a value evaluated in a previous update. The basic setup is that, if a state has changed, it should drive another round of update. And in that update, all component variables should get updated. But if we intentionally reuse an old value, the value can seem to be "skipped" from the update. This way, we can suppress some high-frequency action that is not relevant to the update of the component.

The `useContext` hook is a must-have when it comes to an area update. A `useState` hook can dispatch a state to one place, but it lacks two things. One, it needs to use props to send a state further down to the children, and two, it needs to know which children it sends props to. A context, once established, can be consumed by any child underneath it no matter how deep the level is. And it supports on-demand usage – you use it when you consume it.

The `useRef` hook is a *React*-supported way to bypass the *React* engine. By default, *React* will want to react to all state changes. The `useRef` hook allows you to continue persisting this value without the update capability. So the `useRef` hook can become very handy in places that *React* can't or doesn't allow us to reach.

The preceding hooks aren't the entire *React* collection of hooks. In fact, *React* has more than a dozen built-in hooks; to name some others: `useCallback`, `useLayoutEffect`, `useTransition`, and `useDeferredValue`, and some of them are also in the experimental stage for the future concurrent mode of *React*.

There's one thing unique about the hooks we have covered so far. Each hook is unique and each is designed for an atomic purpose. There's not much overlapping in between. This provides a solid foundation when we want to mix and match them in our application, as we have already seen in previous chapters.

When it comes to building a website, there might be times when you want to create custom logic that might not be covered by these built-in hooks. You might think about extending some of the hooks, or you might even want to rewrite one or two. In that case, what option do we have? The answer to this question is in the next section.

Making a new hook

Can we make a new hook? In each of the previous chapters, we have asked you to read the source code, so by now, you should be familiar with how each is implemented under the hood. So can we follow the same process and create one? Unfortunately, it's not that easy, mostly because this process isn't open for extension on the fly.

Using a game engine as an analogy, it allows you to work with animations, materials, lights, and even game logic, but it doesn't allow you to change the engine. For instance, you can't add a custom identity type that is not animation nor materials and still expect the game engine to pick it up. You might ask "why not?" This is because a custom identity type requires additional implementations for the engine to support it.

> **Note**
>
> *React* is an open source project, which means anyone can contribute to the engine. The source code is also actively maintained by the *Facebook React* team, and they are constantly looking for new proposals and feature requests.

Although the engine is not easily to be extended, the door of creating a custom hook isn't closed. Most of the time, we do not need a new hook type, instead, we want to have a hook with extended behavior. Let's take a look at an example:

```
const aFunctionWrittenByOthers = () => {}
```

Given the preceding function, we can easily encapsulate it in a new function:

```
const aFunction = () => {
  aFunctionWrittenByOthers()
  ...
}
```

A hook is a function. If a hook has been designed to manage a state, whenever we need a state, we don't need to re-invent it; similarly, if a hook has been designed to handle a side effect, whenever we need a side effect, we can adopt these functionalities by invoking it. So, as long as the hook we designed so far is useful and usable enough, we should be able to just use it in our own function. This is the basic idea of reusability.

Let's take a look at the following example:

```
const useUsername = (initialFirst, initialLast) {
  const [firstName, setFirstname] = useState(initialFirst)
  const [lastName, setLastname] = useState(initialLast)
  const fullname = firstName + ' ' + lastName
  return { fullname, setFirstname, setLastname }
}
```

In the preceding function, useUsername uses the useState hook twice, and the output includes a joint fullname from two states, firstName and lastName, as well as two separate dispatch functions to update each of them.

Let's examine the useUsername function a bit more closely, because useUsername is a custom hook.

Writing a custom hook

We can now use the userUsername function we just created as follows:

```
const Title = () => {
  const { fullname } = useUsername('John', 'Doe')
  ...
}
```

Comparing the preceding two versions with or without the useUsername hook, we can see that the useUsername function is more or less an extracted utility function through a code refactoring where the interface for the new useUsername function emerges as two strings as input arguments and an object with a string and two functions as the return value.

This is just how we create a new function in the first place. We create a function because we need it or because we see some duplication in our code, and we can avoid the duplication by doing some refactoring. This way, not only does the code get cleaner afterward, but the function can also be used in some other places in the future. Refactoring is more like a one-stone-shooting-two-birds kind of approach, as long as there're multiple birds to shoot.

This is Computer Science 101, and the custom hook we created so far is one demonstration of it. OK, let's go over some of the basics of the custom hook.

The reason why we call useUsername a custom hook is that it meets the following requirements:

- It is a function.
- It is named with the prefix use.
- It consumes at least one built-in hook.

Apparently, we can write a function and arbitrarily give it a name with the prefix use, but does it qualify as a custom hook? Let's take a look at the following function:

```
const useNotAHook = (a) => {
  return a
}
const Title = () => {
  return useNotAHook()
}
```

A function like useNotAHook in the preceding setup is not a hook! Don't we keep saying a hook is a function? Yes, but not all functions are hooks, even when it gets invoked inside a functional component, such as in the Title component. The useNotAHook is merely a plain function.

You might be thinking "Okay, we need to make a function a bit more complicated to qualify as a custom hook." Let's try with the following function:

```
const useValue = (v) => {
  const [value] = useState(v)
  return value
}
```

There are only two lines in the preceding function, so it's not complicated. It takes the first part of the useState hook and returns the state only. That's it. But is it a custom hook? Yes, it is. So, a custom hook doesn't have to be complicated!

Hopefully, by now, you don't feel dizzy from looking at these mind-bending examples. In short, by convention, a custom hook needs to meet all the requirements listed earlier.

Technically, the only thing that separates the custom hook from a regular function is that it uses at least one of the built-in hooks at least once. What's so special about the built-in hooks? The built-in hooks hook into *React* and provide functionalities that you can't make without opening the engine. The functionalities here mostly refer to managing a persistent state. This is where the name "custom" comes from, to distinguish the hook you created and the built-in ones.

Before we move into creating a custom hook, there's also one more unique thing worth pointing out. Most of the custom hooks are designed without any visual representation attached to them. So, a custom hook is essentially a piece of reusable algorithm.

This is how the *React* team envisioned the hooks can bring to us. Hooks "let you reuse logic between components." Keep this in mind when you create custom hooks. If the logic smells generic enough to you, or at least you think there's one more location where you could apply the same logic, it's time for us to experiment with the idea of using a custom function, and if it turns out it uses one of the built-in hooks, then here you go, you create a custom hook.

Now with the basic idea in mind, retrospectively, if we review the code we have written in this book so far, we would spot that we might have hopped on this boat without knowing it. Let's revisit it.

useToggle

Hooks used in this custom hook: `useState`

Taking one example, we have had this idea of switching a state between `true` and `false` for a while. We use it in switchable cases, such as toggling a checkbox, hovering over a text, raising an error, or anything that simulates a light switch. See *Figure 9.1* for one of the usages:

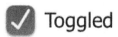

Figure 9.1 – useToggle

Can we abstract this idea to provide such boolean state as well as the toggle functionality? Let's start refactoring:

```
const useToggle = (initialStatus = false) => {
  const [status, setStatus] = useState(initialStatus)
  const toggle = () => {
    dispatch(status => !status)
  )
  return [status, toggle]
}
```

In the preceding code block, the `useToggle` custom hook takes an `initialStatus` as the input argument with `false` as the default value, and it returns the `status` and a `toggle` function. Invoking the `toggle` function flips the `status` from `false` to `true`, or `true` to `false`.

The `useToggle` hook has a very nice function designed with well-defined input arguments and a return value and looks handy for supporting the toggle between a boolean status. There's a small improvement we can make here. Sometimes, we also want to toggle into a specific status instead of the flip:

```
const toggle = (newStatus) => () => {
  if (newStatus === undefined) {
    setState(status => !status)
  } else {
    setState(newStatus)
  }
}
```

In the preceding revised version of `toggle`, when a `newStatus` is given, it toggles to that specific status, otherwise, it flips as in the old `toggle`. Notice we use a double arrow in a row, as in `() => () => {}`:

```
const toggle = (newStatus) => {
    return () => {
        ...
    }
}
```

If we were to write it slowly, we could use the preceding equivalent version where you can clearly see an inline function is returned from a function, since in this case, we expect what's returned from the `toggle` to be an event handler.

A function returning a function is very common in **Functional Programming** (**FP**). Although this book does not cry out for FP (or maybe it already did), it's just natural to use FP in *React* code, especially when working with a function component.

Okay, now we have the custom hook designed, let's give it a spin.

Usages

Say we apply this `useToggle` hook to an `Avatar` component where an `error` can be toggled. The `Avatar` component was introduced in *Chapter 4, Use State to Jumpstart Components*:

```
Const Avatar = ({ src, username }) => {
  const [error, onError] = useToggle()
  return (
    <AvatarStyle>
      {error ? (
        <div>{username}</div>
      ) : (
        <img
          src={src}
          alt={username}
          onError={onError()}
        />
      )}
    </AvatarStyle>
  )
}
```

Interesting! Though there's no drastic difference before and after applying the useToggle, the logic becomes quite clear in that an error state gets toggled after the image loading runs into an error.

> **Playground – Avatar with useToggle**
>
> Feel free to play with this online example at https://codepen.io/ windmaomao/pen/yLozOJQ.

Let's try to apply useToggle in another place, such as the Tooltip component, also introduced in *Chapter 4, Use State to Jumpstart Components*:

```
const Tooltip = ({ children, tooltip }) => {
  const [entered, onEntered] = useToggle()
  return (
    <TooltipStyle>
      <div
        onMouseEnter={onEntered(true)}
        onMouseLeave={onEntered(false)}
      >
        {children}
      </div>
      {entered && (
        <div className="__tooltip">
          {tooltip}
        </div>
      )}
    </TooltipStyle>
  )
```

In the preceding code, we used a useToggle to return an entered state and an onEntered function that feeds into the onMouseEnter and onMouseLeave event handler neatly.

> **Playground – Tooltip with useToggle**
>
> Feel free to play with this online example at https://codepen.io/ windmaomao/pen/QWMqNKx.

The concept of having a toggle mechanism is revealed vividly via the useToggle hook. The function can be tested separately and can be extended with relatively little effort. If we use this hook often, the cost of creating it and maintaining it can become even cheaper.

References

There are a number of people who have written similar hooks to `useToggle` on the internet. Here is a list of some of them as references in case you'd like to learn more about this custom hook:

- `useToggle`: `https://usehooks.com/useToggle/`.

- `react-use-toggle`: `https://github.com/bsonntag/react-use-toggle`. It has a good test written.

useWindow

Hooks used in this custom hook: `useState` and `useEffect`

A text or image can adjust its appearance based on the current browser window size. We experimented with this idea in *Chapter 5, Use Effect to Handle Side Effects*. See *Figure 9.2*.

Figure 9.2 – useWindow custom hook

Now the question is: can we abstract this idea out and apply it to anything on the screen as in a responsive design? Let's refactor the code a bit to come up with a custom `useWindow` hook:

```
const useWindow = (size = 0) => {
  const [width, setWidth] = useState(0)
  useEffect(() => {
    function handleResize() {
      setWidth(window.innerWidth)
    }
    handleResize()
    window.addEventListener("resize", handleResize)
    return () => {
      window.removeEventListener("resize", handleResize)
    }
  }, [setWidth])
  return [width, width > size]
}
```

The preceding `useWindow` hook is taken out of our previous code and returns the current width of the screen. A `useEffect` is used to handle the initialization and cleanup of the system event upon a browser `resize`. During each screen resize, the window's `innerWidth` is stored in the `width` state.

In order to make it easy to use, we can provide the input argument `size` to this custom hook, so that it can also tell us whether the `width` is beyond that `size`, telling us whether the screen is wide enough to support a large-sized version.

Usages

Let's apply this custom hook to a text that can adjust to a large version when the screen size reaches beyond 600 *px*:

```
const Greeting = () => {
  const [, wide] = useWindow(600)
  return <h1>{wide ? "Hello World" : "Hello"}</h1>
}
```

This looks very easy to use, and moreover, the functionalities pertaining to detecting the window size are entirely taken out and outsourced to the `useWindow` hook, therefore reducing the code quite a bit.

> **Playground – Responsive with useWindow**
>
> Feel free to play with this online example at `https://codepen.io/windmaomao/pen/zYdEqog`.

There's one unique thing about this custom hook. Unlike a classical `media-query` supported by *CSS*, the `wide` flag returned from `useWindow` is used to change the layout entirely. This means we can support a very drastic screen change to accommodate the screen size:

```
const Header = () => {
  const [, wide] = useWindow(725)
  return wide ? <HeaderWide /> : <HeaderMini />
}
```

In the preceding code, `HeaderWide` and `HeaderMini` are two completely different layout components to display a header for screen sizes of less than 725 and larger than 725.

One thing we learned from making this custom hook is that the functionalities can be tailored to your own purpose. Here, we export a flag, `width > size`, because we believe it's useful for the current project. However, the responsiveness setting isn't fixed, and it can vary from project to project. This doesn't stop us from creating something useful at the moment. And this is the point of code refactoring, to improve the quality of the code.

References

Our version of `useWindow` monitors the window width only, but we can track both the width and height of the screen, as implemented in the following references:

- `useWindowSize`: https://usehooks.com/useWindowSize/
- `useWindowSize`: https://github.com/jaredLunde/react-hook/tree/master/packages/window-size

useAsync

Hooks used in this custom hook: `useState`, `useEffect`, `useRef`, and `useMemo`

One hook everyone wants to get their hands dirty with is `useAsync`, which is used to fetch an async resource as we introduced in *Chapter 5, Use Effect to Handle Side Effects*. See *Figure 9.3*:

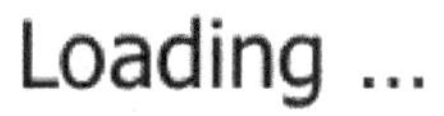

Loading ...

Figure 9.3 – useAsync hook

As simple as it sounds, everyone comes with different requirements and implementations for their projects. Here are a few features that we would like to have:

- Support a loading indicator.
- Can execute on demand.
- Support error handling.
- Can cancel async call.
- Can cache async data.

The feature list can go on and on. In this book, I will provide a basic version that supports the first two items.

At any point, the call should be aware of the `loading` state, and when the resource is resolved, the `data` should be available to use. Also, we'd like to keep a handle on the `execute` function in case we want to fetch the resource again. Let's design it in a custom hook:

```
const useAsync = (
  asyncFunc,
  initialParams = {},
  immediate = true
) => {
  ...
  return { execute, loading, data }
}
```

In the preceding code block, the `useAsync` hook takes three input arguments, `asyncFunc`, `initialParams`, and `immediate`, and returns three properties, `execute`, `loading`, and `data`. The `asyncFunc` function is a user-provided async function, such as a *Promise*, defined as follows:

```
const fn = ({ id }) => {
  return fetch('/anAPIResource/${id}')
    .then(res => res.json())
}
```

In the preceding `fn` promise, an `id` is sent as the input argument. This is where the second input argument of `useAsync` becomes useful, and it can be used to provide the `initialParams` in key/value pairs as in `{ id: 3 }`.

The `useAsync` hook also supports an optional flag, `immediate`, and when set as `true`, it invokes the async call immediately after the component mount. Although this is the most popular case, we can set it as `false` so we manually invoke `execute` later.

Inside the hook, we use states to model `loading` and `data`:

```
const [loading, setLoading] = useState(immediate)
const [data, setData] = useState(null)
const mountedRef = useRef(true)
```

A `useRef` is used for `mountedRef` to know when this component is dismounted; we explained this in *Chapter 8, Use Ref to Hide Stuff*.

To provide the capability of fetching the resource on demand, an `execute` function is created and accepts a `params` object:

```
const execute = params => {
  setLoading(true)
```

```
    return asyncFunc({
      ...initialParams,
      ...params
    }).then(res => {
      if (!mountedRef.current) return null
      setData(res)
      setLoading(false)
      return res
    })
}
```

The preceding execute function sets the loading to true so that if we have a spinner wired with it, it can start to spin. And then it invokes the asyncFunc with the combination of params and initialParams so the params can overwrite any keys set by initialParams.

When the resource is resolved and returned, we first check if the component is still mounted by mountedRef, and if not, we skip to avoid the memory leak. Otherwise, it sets the data accordingly and dismisses the spinner by setting loading to false.

There's also a subtlety here that we want to use one version of this execute function instead of a new instance in each update, therefore, we can apply useMemo here to make that happen:

```
const execute = useMemo(() => params => {
  setLoading(true)
  return …
}, [asyncFunc, setData, setLoading])
```

When immediate is set to true, we want to invoke the fetch right after the mount and this is supported through a useEffect hook:

```
useEffect(() => {
  if (immediate) {
    execute(initialParams)
  }
}, [immediate, execute])
```

To make sure we don't run into a memory leak, we also need to set the mountedRef to false when it's unmounted. This is done through another useEffect:

```
useEffect(() => {
  return () => {
    mountedRef.current = false
  }
}, [mountedRef])
```

With these changes, this custom `useAsync` hook is quite feature-rich for fetching a resource in general. Let's give it a spin.

Usages

Now let's apply the `useAsync` custom hook to a `Title` component and see how we can preload some info from an *API*:

```
const fn = () => fetch("google.com")
const Title = () => {
  const { data, loading } = useAsync(fn)
  if (loading) return 'loading ...'
  if (!data) return null
  return <div>loaded</div>
}
```

In the preceding code, the async function is invoked immediately. After the mount, it displays `null`, and during the fetching, it displays `loading...`, and displays `loaded` after the fetch is successful. In this simple case, we added two short circuit pathways:

```
if (loading) return 'loading ...'
```

Upon loading, we switch to a loading status; this is the place where you can install a pretty (inline) loader or spinner:

```
const spinner = <Spinner >
...
if (loading) return spinner
```

Regardless of whether the loading hasn't started or the fetch has failed, as long as the data isn't available, we display nothing on the screen:

```
if (!data) return null
```

This logic is effective to prevent the user from seeing any incomplete or wrong data.

> **Playground – Fetch with useAsync**
>
> Feel free to play with this online example at `https://codepen.io/windmaomao/pen/jOLaOxO`.

Okay, let's try a case without fetching initially. Instead, we fetch a resource of an arbitrary id from a user interaction, such as a **Delete** button in a table row:

```
const fn = ({ id }) => fetch('google.com/${id}')
const Title = () => {
  const {
    execute, data, loading
  } = useAsync(fn, {}, false)
  const onClick = id => () => {
    execute({ id })
  }
  if (loading) return 'loading ...'
  return data ? <h1>{data}</h1> : (
    <button onClick={onClick(3)}>Load 3</button>
  )
}
```

In the preceding example, the fetch promise is amended to accept id as input. We used execute manually inside an event handler, onClick, where we fetched the resource with a given id.

Playground – Manual Fetch with useAsync

Feel free to play with this online example at https://codepen.io/windmaomao/pen/GRvOgoa.

References

The useAsync hook we provided here serves as a basic template for learning purposes. If you are interested in more functionalities to serve your project needs, you can find more at the following references:

- useAsync: https://usehooks.com/useAsync/
- Hooks Async: https://github.com/dai-shi/react-hooks-async
- Fetching Library: https://github.com/marcin-piela/react-fetching-library
- Vercel SWR: https://swr.vercel.app/ – supports caching and server integration
- React Query: https://github.com/tannerlinsley/react-query

useDebounced

Hooks used in this custom hook: `useState`, `useEffect`, and `useRef`

In *Chapter 6, Use Memo to Boost Performance*, we ran into a very interesting implementation where we debounced the user keystroke so that we don't invoke a heavy operation (such as search) too frequently.

Figure 9.4 – useDebounced hook

A pattern that emerged is that for a given state, whenever we change it via dispatch, we want to wait for a period of time before we are assured that it's the right time to act upon it. So essentially we want to design a new state as a debounced version of a given state. Let's try to capture this pattern in a custom `useDebounced` hook:

```
const useDebounced = (oldState, duration) => {
  const [state, dispatch] = useState(oldState)
  const invokeRef = useRef(null)
  useEffect(() => {
    invokeRef.current = setTimeout(() => {
      dispatch(oldState)
    }, duration)
    return () => {
      clearTimeout(invokeRef.current)
    }
  }, [oldState, duration])
  return state
}
```

In the preceding code block, the `useDebounced` hook is designed to take two input arguments, the `oldState` and the time `duration` for the debounce duration. The hook returns a new `state` with a debounced value.

It actually can't reuse the `debounce` function from the *Lodash* library, so the `debounce` functionality is recreated here. The frequency of the new state is controlled by a `useEffect`. Upon each change from `oldState`, it kicks off a `setTimeout`, which is asking to run a callback after a certain `duration`.

Here, we used a `useRef` to make sure we can keep track of a persistent function handle for `setTimeout` during the lifetime of the component. Between now and the duration ends, if another change comes in, it cancels the previous `setTimeout` via `clearTimeout`, thus preventing the change to apply to the `state`. Only when one of the `setTimeout` manages to get invoked does the change of `oldState` get applied to `state`.

In a way, the `oldState` and the `state` lags a bit in between. Let's give it a spin and see how we can use this `useDebounced` hook.

Usages

Let's take a look at how it's used in the `Title` component where we need to perform a search based on the user typing:

```
const Title = () => {
  const [text, setText] = useState('')
  const query = useDebounced(text, 300)
  const matched = useMemo(() => {
    return fruites.filter(v => v.includes(query))
  }, [query])
  const onChange = e => {
    const t = e.target.value
    setText(t)
  }
  return (
    <>
      <input value={text} onChange={onChange} />
      {matched.join(',')}
    </>
  )
}
```

In the preceding code, a `text` state is sent to `useDebounced` to form a new `query` state:

```
const query = useDebounced(text, 300)
```

Because the `query` state is less frequently updated, we can wire it to the `filter` via `useMemo`, since otherwise, the `text` state can get updated very rapidly via `onChange`. In a way, we created a state event out of `query` so the *UI* updates according to two data streams with different frequencies.

> **Playground – Search with useDebounced**
>
> Feel free to play with this online example at `https://codepen.io/windmaomao/pen/bGrYNmB`.

From this `useDebounced` custom hook, we can see an artificial event created out of listening to a state change that can be as useful as a physical event.

References

To learn more about the `useDebounced` hook, here are the reference links for you:

- useDebounce: `https://usehooks.com/useDebounce/`.
- useDebounce: `https://github.com/xnimorz/use-debounce`. This supports all debounce options.

useClickOutside

Hooks used in this custom hook: `useEffect`

In *Chapter 8, Use Ref to Hide Stuff*, we learned about a case where we can detect when a user clicks outside a component. This feature is pretty generic and we want to take advantage of this in various parts of the project, such as dismissing a modal or tooltip – see *Figure 9.5*.

Figure 9.5 – useClickOutside hook

Let's see if we can refactor the old code a bit and turn it into a custom `useClickOutside` hook:

```
function useClickOutside(ref, handler) {
  useEffect(() => {
    const evt = e => {
      if (!ref.current) return
      if (!ref.current.contains(e.target)) {
        handler && handler()
      }
```

```
    }
    window.addEventListener("mousedown", evt)
    return () => {
      window.removeEventListener("mousedown", evt)
    }
  }, [ref, handler])
}
```

The useClickOutside hook accepts two input arguments, the first one is a ref to the element, and the second is the callback handler to invoke after detecting clicking outside. Notice the hook doesn't return any value.

A useEffect is used to manage a mousedown event, and if the click is inside the component, the handler is prevented from being invoked. We basically take our old code into a separate function. Let's give it a spin.

Usages

We can try out the useClickOutside on a Menu component:

```
const Menu = ({ on, dismiss }) => {
  const ref= useRef()
  useClickOutside(ref, toggle(false))
  if (!on) return null
  return (
    <ul ref={ref}>
      <li>Home</li>
      <li>Price</li>
      <li>Product</li>
      <li>Support</li>
      <li>About</li>
    </ul>
  )
}
```

This time we set up the Menu to support two input arguments. One is the on flag and the other is the dismiss function. Both are provided via props so the Menu can be driven by the parent component:

```
const App = () => {
  const [on, toggle] = useToggle(true)
  return (
    <Menu
      on={on}
      dismiss={toggle(false)}
```

```
      </>
    )
  }
```

In the preceding App component, we used an on state from a custom hook we just built earlier to provide us with a boolean as well as a toggle function. We used them to drive a Menu. Cool, we started using our own custom hook in no time. Initially, the on is set to true, indicating the Menu is displayed. Clicking anywhere outside of it would dismiss it.

> **Playground – Menu with useClickOutside**
>
> Feel free to play with this online example at https://codepen.io/
> windmaomao/pen/qBXVdOe.

References

To learn more about the useClickOutside hook, here are some reference links for you:

- useOnClickOutside: https://usehooks.com/useOnClickOutside/

- useClickOutside: https://github.com/ElForastero/use-click-outside

useCurrent

Built-in hooks used in this custom hook: useState

When using the useState, we encountered quite a few issues that prevented a newcomer from understanding how to use it properly, mainly from the inherited laggy behavior due to the fact that the state value does not change right after the dispatch.

```
const [state, dispatchState] = useState(0)
```

In the preceding line, if we understand the dispatchState function is to dispatch and request a change, then there's not much we need to do because that's how *React* designs the useState. However, most often we tend to think differently:

```
const [state, setState] = useState(0)
```

The preceding setState name is the main reason we push ourselves into trouble, because here we would expect the state to change right after the setState statement.

In *Chapter 8, Use Ref to Hide Stuff*, we used a useRef to locate the current value. There are two different ways to solve this problem: one is to design a container to keep pointing to the current value, the other is to design an access function to give us the current one when needed. Let's give the second method a shot this time:

```
function useCurrent(initialState) {
  const [obj, setObj] = useState({ state: initialState })
  const dispatch = newState => {
    if (obj.state !== newState) {
      obj.state = newState
      setObj({ ...obj })
    }
  }
  const getState = () => obj.state
  return [getState, dispatch]
}
```

In the preceding custom useCurrent hook, it stores the state under a state property of an obj. When you need to find out the state, you can invoke getState function, and when you need to update the state, you perform dispatch as used to be. Here, we have to manage the obj manually, and if we find out the newState is not different than the current obj.state, we skip this dispatch.

Usages

Let's give it a spin for our 3-second-delayed clicks example:

```
const Title = () => {
  const [getCount, setCount] = useCurrent(0)
  const onClick = () => {
    setTimeout(() => {
      setCount(getCount() + 1)
    }, 3000)
  }
  return <button onClick={onClick}>{getCount()}</button>
}
```

The preceding code shows that this time, the code is simplified a bit since we don't need a ref to track the current value. Instead, we use a custom useCurrent to manage the state. The big difference is that anytime we need to find out the count, we need to invoke getCount returned from the hook. The plus side is that we don't have to always wonder what the current count is anymore.

> **Playground – Current State with useCurrent**
>
> Feel free to play with this online example at `https://codepen.io/windmaomao/pen/VwzrvBX`.

References

Check these links out to see how people approach this problem from different angles:

- Use Ref State: `https://scastiel.dev/posts/2019-02-19-react-hooks-get-current-state-back-to-the-future/`.

- `useStateRef`: `https://github.com/Aminadav/react-useStateRef`

- `useRefState`: `https://github.com/alex-cory/urs`.

- Use Safe State: `https://ahooks.js.org/hooks/advanced/use-safe-state/`. This implements a safe state.

useProxy

Built-in hooks used in this custom hook: `useState`, `useEffect`, and `useRef`

The thinking behind either fixing or improving the *React* state never ends. One cool idea originates from the question "why can't we just do a plain assignment for states instead of using the dispatch approach?" One of the technical issues blocking us is that the assignment can't be done unless there's an object or something to hold the state. So, if we were to allow the storing of properties under an object like so:

```
const p = useProxy({ count: 0, text: '' })
```

Then we could turn a dispatch into an assignment like the following:

```
p.count++
p.text = 'Hello World'
```

Let's take a look at how we can design such things with the help of the *Proxy* introduced by *ES6*:

```
const useProxy = (initialObj) => {
  const [,dispatch] = useState(initialObj)
  const [obj] = useState(new Proxy(initialObj, {
    get: function() {
      return Reflect.get(...arguments)
    },
    set: function(obj, prop, value) {
```

```
      if (obj[prop] !== value) {
        obj[prop] = value
        dispatch({ ...obj })
      }
      return true
    }
  }))
  return obj
}
```

The preceding custom `useProxy` hook takes a similar approach as the `useCurrent` hook and stores the `initialObj` into a state but at the same time creates another special object with the Proxy. Without going into too much detail about the Proxy usage, the special object basically captures the moment of reading and writing any property into two function calls, `get` and `set`. Here, we don't really care about the `get` so it reverts to the default behavior, whereas the `set` overrides the default behavior with a new version:

```
set: function(obj, prop, value) {
  if (obj[prop] !== value) {
    obj[prop] = value
    dispatch({ ...obj })
  }
  return true
}
```

The preceding code gets invoked for any statement like `obj.prop = value`. The implementation is quite similar to that of the `getCurrent` hook, where it checks if the new `value` is any different than the stored `obj[prop]` and makes a dispatch if that's the case.

Since we are tracking a couple of states under the properties with an object, it's worthwhile adding a `mountRef` flag in case things go wrong after the component is dismounted:

```
const useProxy = (initialObj) => {
  ...
  const mountRef = useRef(true)
  useEffect(() => {
    return () => {
      mountRef.current = false
    }
  })
  ...
}
```

Given a mountRef, we can modify the set to disable it to avoid a memory leak:

```
set: function(obj, prop, value) {
  if (!mountedRef.current) return false
  ...
}
```

Okay, with all these features built, let's put them together and give them a spin.

Usages

The useProxy hook is a lot more powerful , but it requires you to put all values under an object and it can be really useful especially for form handling:

```
const Form = () => {
  const form = useProxy({ count: 0, text: '' })
```

In the preceding Form component, we define a form object to hold two states, count and text. Let's first take a look how we can increment a number now:

```
const onClick = () => { ++form.count }
return (
  <div>
    <h1>Count: { form.count }</h1>
    <button onClick={onClick}>Increment</button>
  </div>
)
```

In the preceding code, the count is displayed from form.count, but when it comes to incrementing it, we simply do ++form.count. Essentially, this is equivalent to either of the following:

```
form.count += 1
from.count = form.count + 1
```

From the usage experience, we don't have to remember what a dispatch is; all we need to do is a plain assignment. The custom useProxy hook takes care of the dispatch for us.

There's another advantage coming from this custom hook, that is, from now on, both set and get are done through the same object, form. This means if we need to ask a child to handle one form element, we do not have to send two pieces as we normally do. Let's take a look at one example with the other text state:

```
const Text = (({ form }) => {
  const onChange = e => {
    form.text = e.target.value
```

```
  }
  return (
    <input
      value={form.text}
      onChange={onChange}
    />
  )
})
const Form = () => {
  const form = useProxy({ count: 0, text: '' })
  return(
    <div>
      <Text form={form} />
    </div>
  )
}
```

In the preceding example, we define a `Text` component to handle the text input. Notice we only need to send the `form` through a prop. And inside the `Text` component, both the display and assignment of this text are managed via `form.text`. Crazily handy, isn't it?

> **Playground – Form with useProxy**
>
> Feel free to play with this online example at `https://codepen.io/windmaomao/pen/eYEeZmL`.

The `useProxy` hook does ask us to use an object to manage states, but once you are onboard with this approach, you might feel more like coding normally without the *React* state hassle.

References

- Valtio: `https://github.com/pmndrs/valtio`
- Use State Proxy: `https://github.com/beenotung/use-state-proxy`
- Proxy States: `https://github.com/windmaomao/proxy-state`

Summary

In this chapter, we summarized all the *React* built-in hooks that we've introduced so far and then went on to how to create a custom hook. Then, once we understood the concept, we went over all the code we wrote in this book and turned some of it into custom hooks, including `useToggle`, `useWindow`, `useAsync`, `useDebounced`, `useClickOutside`, `useCurrent`, and `useProxy`.

In the next chapter, we will get to know how *React* pulls together all different types of web resources and orchestrates them to build a website.

Questions and answers

Here are some questions and answers to refresh your knowledge:

1. What are *React* built-in hooks?

    React built-in hooks refers to all hooks designed by *React*, including `useState`, `useEffect`, and so on. You can't create a built-in hook on the fly, but you can contribute your idea and send a pull request to the *React* core team to review.

2. What is a custom hook?

    We can create a custom hook by consuming one of the *React* built-in hooks and giving the hook name prefixed with `use`. A custom hook can be as powerful as a built-in hook. The purpose of the built-in hook is to address atomic core capability whereas the custom hook is normally created to address practical project problems. There're hundreds of custom hooks on the internet you might find useful or inspiring.

3. What's the best practice for creating a hook?

    A custom hook can be, and most times is, created naturally out of the code refactoring process. As long as you feel a bundle of code can be reused involving a hook, that's the time you can extract those functionalities out and make it generic to be referenced by other parts of the project. In a way, you can think of a custom hook as a utility function, except it involves a built-in hook.

10
Building a Website with React

In this last chapter of this book, we will talk about *React* in general, especially the role that *React* plays in web development. We will approach this topic from three aspects to see how *React* puts resources together to build a site. First, we will take a look at how *React* embraces new *JavaScript ES6* features, such as arrow function and template strings. Then, we will walk through how a component can be styled using a *CSS-in-JS* approach via libraries such as `styled-JSX` and `styled-components`. Last, but not least, we will also get to know JSX code and how it is used to transform the *HTML*-like lines into *JavaScript* expressions.

We will cover the following topics in this chapter:

- The function of *React*
- Embracing *JavaScript ES6*
- Adopting CSS-in-JS approach
- Going from *HTML* to JSX
- Questions and answers

Exploring functions of React

In this section, we will start with an exploration of the function React serves in the website development field. By doing that we hope to get a more accurate description about how React can help us.

The book has been dedicated to introducing a state into a function component under *React*, especially the hook mechanism. We hope that by reading this book, you get to know how to design hooks in the right way.

When comparing *React* to other UI frameworks, have you heard that sometimes people refer to it as a utility rather than a framework? There's no clear definition of what should be called a framework and what shouldn't. Judging by the amount of *React* source code and how it wires with other systems, we can hardly treat it as a utility library. But at the same time, we also should remember the goal that *React* established with in the first place, because knowing this will help you to use this technology in the right way. Let's take a look at the usage:

```
const rootEl = document.getElementById('root')
ReactDOM.render(<App />, rootEl)
```

The preceding code is how we start all *React* projects. It searches for a *DOM* element and renders a component under it. Moreover, afterward, the screen under that element gets "managed" by *React*. This means that *React* overwrites everything under that element and refreshes upon any state change inside the component.

Therefore, the preceding `ReactDOM.render` method is the line to integrate *React* with your project. As you see, this line is powerful. In fact, it can be used multiple times for one project. Consider the following *HTML* page:

```
<div class="slider" value="3">loading...</div>
<div cla"s="sli"er" val"e""5">loading...</div>
```

Instead of controlling the whole site, we want to replace each `slider` instance with something more feature-rich:

```
const elements = document.querySelectorA'l('.sli'er')
elements.forEach(el => {
  const value = el.getAttribu'e('va'ue')
  ReactDOM.render(<Slider value={value} />, el)
})
```

We can go through the elements matching the `slider` instance in the *HTML*. For each element found, we take its `value` attribute and send it to a component with `ReactDOM.render`. Wow! All sliders are managed by *React*.

Although having multiple `render` instances is not a typical approach, we build a **Single Page Application (SPA)**. This does give us one important message; that is, from the technical aspect, the goal of *React* is to replace and manage *DOM* elements on the screen. To make this happen, a new root fiber is created internally for each element so the engine knows where to start updating when a dispatch arrives.

We know by now what *React* is designed to do. Let's take a quick look at how much effort it takes to do this – for instance, what are all the dependencies to invoke the `render` statement?

```
const { render } = require('react-dom')
```

To kick off the engine, we need a `render` function provided by the `react-dom` package. The component can be designed somewhere else, which requires the utilities of the `react` package, such as `createElement` and `useState`:

```
const { createElement, useState } = require('react')
const Slider = () => {
  const [value] = useState(0)
  ...
}
```

Other than `react-dom` and `react` packages, it's the `document` object that we need to locate and manipulate the *DOM* element. But normally, as long as we have a browser session, we assume the `document` is available.

In short, there are two dependency packages. The `react` package is used for defining a component. With it, the component definition can be output into a format that the engine can understand. The `react-dom` package is used to render and manage the component to the screen. This means that before you kick off the engine, you don't need `react-dom`. Most of the development time is spent using the `react` package to define our components. From this exercise, we should clearly see the function of *React* as a utility library.

To build a website with *React*, we need to do all the things that a web developer needs to do, that is, designing the site layout with *HTML*, making the site look beautiful with *CSS*, and adding business logic and interaction to engage the user with *JavaScript*. So, the question becomes how all these building blocks fit in the new component ecosystem. Let's take a look at them one at a time.

Embracing JavaScript ES6

React is written in the *JavaScript* language. *JavaScript* has been evolving for the past 20 years. With usage in frameworks such as jQuery, Angular, *React*, and Node.js, *JavaScript* is one of the most popular and influential programming languages.

The latest *JavaScript* is based on ECMAScript 2015, which is also known as *ES6*. This brought a few important features to *JavaScript*, and *React* has quickly adopted these features quite nicely. The following are just a few of the features:

- Arrow function
- Spread and rest
- Object enhancement
- Template strings
- Destructuring
- Let and const
- Modules
- Symbols

If you are considering using *JavaScript* as your main language, it's recommended that in your free time, you go over all the preceding materials because they are commonly used by *React* apps. We'll go over each of these features in the following sections.

Arrow function

The arrow function is a new syntax for function expressions. A typical function can be defined with a `function` keyword:

```
function abc(v) {
}
```

ES6 introduces a more compact way of defining the preceding function with an arrow (`=>`):

```
const abc = v => {
}
```

The preceding arrow version omits the word `function` and makes a function look more like an object. The arrow function is often used as a callback:

```
arr.map(v => v * 2)
```

The preceding code returns a new array with each element doubled. When we make a dispatch in *React*, we also tend to use the arrow syntax:

```
setCount(v => v + 1)
```

Note that the `return` statement can be omitted if the arrow function returns a single expression. We can compare the preceding line with the regular function form:

```
setCount(function (v) {
  return v + 1
})
```

It's apparent that the arrow function tends to be compact while working as an object. Being an object implies that we can pass it freely to anywhere via a function input argument. Sometimes, you also see a chained version, as follows:

```
const fn = a => b => a + b
```

The preceding line is equivalent to the following:

```
const fn = (a) => {
  return (b) => {
    return a + b
  }
}
```

You may find the arrow function quite expressive. The book basically uses this format solely. Only in one case does the book revert to the regular function format:

```
fn()
function fn() {
}
```

We can invoke the function before the declaration in general, the compiler wouldn't complain. However, this wouldn't work for the arrow function:

```
fn()
const fn = () => {
}
```

This is because `fn` needs to be declared first before it can be referenced.

The arrow function, though more compact and expressive, does carry some caveats compared to the regular function:

- It sets the `this` object upon creation instead of invocation.
- It does not set the `arguments` object after invocation.
- It cannot be used as a `constructor` function.

Spread and rest

Pretty new to the *Javascript* language, spread is a way to express all the parts of an item, and rest is a way to express the rest of the part of an item apart from the first few parts.

ES6 introduces quite a few features to allow our code to be more expressive. One of the features is to use a . . . keyword, as hardly anybody bothers to remember the exact feature name. Let's take a look at one example:

```
const a = [1, 2, 3, 4, 5]
const b = [...a, 6]
```

In the preceding code, the b variable gets all the elements from the a array, spreads them into five elements, and then appends the new element so that the new array carries six elements in total. You can use this with an object as well:

```
const a = { first: 'John', last: 'Doe' }
const b = { ...a, age: 23 }
```

In the preceding code, the b variable gets all the properties from the a object, spreads them, and then adds the new `age` property so that the new object carries three properties in total.

Note that both usages of the spread operator create a new variable, either an array or an object. When it comes to quickly creating another variable out of an existing variable, this new syntax becomes quite popular.

React uses this feature quite often in component design:

```
const App = ({ title, ...props }) => {
  return <div {...props}>Hello</div>
}j
```

The preceding component uses the `props` object to capture a list of props other than `title`. This becomes useful for the following reasons:

- We do not have to care about the number of other props present in the list.

- We can send this list further down into the children component.

There's another similar *ES6* feature called the `rest` operator which behaves similarly to the `spread` operator. This is when . . . is applied to a function's input argument list:

```
function abc(a, b, ...rest) {
}
abc(a, b, 1)        // rest = [1]
abc(a, b, 1, 2)   // rest = [1, 2]
```

In the preceding `abc` function, we used a . . . rest operator to obtain additional arguments.. The `rest` variable holds an array, and when we invoke the function with more than two arguments, the additional arguments get populated into this array.

Object enhancement

With *ES6*, an object is extended to support quite a few features. Let's take a look at some of them. One of the features is that we can use a shorthand version while making an assignment to a property under an object:

```
const first = "John"
const last = "Doe"
const name = { first, last }
```

If we write the preceding code in the old way, it would be equivalent to the following:

```
const name = { first: first, last: last }
```

If the property name matches the assignment variable name, *ES6* allows us to write the property name only once. This becomes handy in practice, and because of this, it's common to see people take advantage of it by creating a temporary variable to match with the property name:

```
const onClick = () => {
  const first = "John"
  const name = { first }
}
```

Another enhancement to an object is to support an expression as the property name:

```
const name = e.target.name
const value = e.target.value
return { [name]: value }
```

The preceding code is what we write to support a form submission. Don't confuse the last line of that code with the following version:

```
return { name: value }
```

Note that the difference between these two is the bracket around name. Without the bracket, name would assign the value to the "name" property. However, in the [name] version, it would assign the value to a property with a name stored in a name variable. If name carries a "first" word, then the [name] version would become the following:

```
return { first: value }
```

Basically, this enables us to use any *JavaScript* expression as the property key. This was not possible before, so we used to write the following to remedy the issue:

```
obj[name] = value
```

Template strings

It used to be cumbersome to construct a long string in *JavaScript* without sacrificing the raw format of the string. To address this problem, *ES6* added the template strings, which allow a string to be enclosed by the back-tick ('), a strange character that we use often when working with *Markdown* files. With this syntax, a string can be written in the following way:

```
'This is a string'
```

What's interesting about the template, beyond the regular quoted string using " or ', is that it supports a paragraph of text written across multiple lines while preserving the line breaks:

```
'
This
is
a
string
'
```

This makes it useful when we want to introduce a paragraph of long text without formatting its content. The template strings also work with any *JavaScript* expression:

```
const what = "This"
const str = '
${what}
is
a
string
'
```

In the preceding code, we replaced the incidence of ${what} with the "This" string in the template. Essentially, what's written inside ${ } can be any *JavaScript* expression.

One common usage of the template strings is to convert another format into a string:

```
const n = 3
const str = '${n}'
const url = 'http://foo.org/bar?id=${n}'
```

You can see in the preceding code that this becomes handy when we need to assemble a string such as a dynamic url.

We can apply the preceding code to a more complex version, such as the *CSS* content:

```
const color = 'red'
const Button = css'
  display: inline-block;
  color: ${color};
'
```

The preceding code uses a different form called tagged templates, and css is what's referred to as a tagged function. Here's another example:

```
function image(strings) {
  return '<img src="${strings[0]" />'
}
const s = image'
  http://google.com
'
```

The preceding code defines an image tagged function, which transforms strings into another format – in our case, an image element statement. From this, you can see that tagged templates can be useful as a utility to alleviate the pain of generating strings. In the *Adopting CSS-in-JS* approach section that follows, we shall see more examples of this.

Destructuring

The word "destructuring" is an awkward word to say and maybe we can't even find it in the dictionary.

However, you might have used this feature quite a few times in the past:

```
const arr = [1, 2, 3]
const [a, b] = arr
```

Essentially, destructuring allows you to destruct an object and assign the dissembled elements to variables. The preceding code is destructuring usage applied to an array, which is equivalent to the following:

```
const a = arr[0]
const b = arr[1]
```

You can see that during the destructuring process, we follow the given structure to select the needed elements. Similarly, it can be applied to an object:

```
const name = { first: 'John', last: 'Doe' }
const { first, last } = name
```

The preceding statement translates to the following:

```
const first = name.first
const last = name.last
```

Although we can continue to use the old method, destructuring is much easier and quicker to use. Keep in mind that the element you select has to exist; otherwise, you can get an undefined, as shown in the following case:

```
const name = { first: 'John' }
const { second } = name
```

Another useful feature with destructuring is that you can rename a property if you want to store it under another name:

```
const { first: firstName } = name
```

The preceding line translates to the following:

```
const firstName = name.first
```

Essentially, the `firstName` variable is used for the assignment instead of `first`, even though `first` is the property name under the object.

Quite often, destructuring is used in combination with other *ES6* features, such as the spread operator:

```
const { first } = { ...name, last }
```

We see this preceding statement quite often in *React* code, so let me explain each part of it:

- `...name` is to spread all properties of the `name` object.
- `last` is the enhanced object syntax to add the `last` property.
- `{ ...name, last }` creates a new object out of the existing one.
- `first` is destructuring the `first` property out of the new object.

Wow, there's a lot going on! Maybe we can write it in an equivalent version using the old method:

```
const temp = Object.assign({}, name)
temp.last = last
const first = temp.first
```

Essentially, the new syntax takes only one line instead of three lines, but shockingly the outcome is much more accurate and expressive.

If you are new to this feature, don't hesitate in slowing down a bit while composing each part. The reason for that is, you will not only gain knowledge on what the new syntax provides but also you won't miss any logic accidentally.

let and const

Using *JavaScript* in the past, you may have been confused by the `var`, `let`, and `const` keywords. Which one are you supposed to use to declare a variable?

One thing to first get out of way is that `var` isn't used often anymore; it's there mostly for backward compatibility because it uses a strange scope rule. Instead, we should all use `let` and `const` because they are based on block scopes that developers are more comfortable using:

```
function abc() {
  let a = 1
  if (true) {
    const b = 2
    for (let i = 1; i < 3; i++) {
```

```
      . . .
    }
  }
}
```

In the preceding code, the a variable lives in the scope of the function and the b variable lives in the scope of the condition statement. Both references are valid in the scope specified by the { } parent enclosing block. If you try to reference either a or b outside of their defined scope, the compiler now throws an error. The same applies to the i variable, defined using let under the loop. If we had used var, it would make i accessible within the entire function body.

As the names imply, you use let for a variable that needs to change later on and const for things you don't expect to change. Here's an example:

```
let x = 5
x = 6                // valid
const n = "abc"
n = "def"            // compiler error
```

In the preceding code, if you change x to 6 later on, it's totally fine. But the compiler will raise an error if you try to change n to "def". This applies to any primitive value, such as a number or a string.

When it comes to a non-primitive value, such as an object or an array, it gets a bit complicated:

```
let obj = { a: 1, b: 2 }
const obj = { a: 1, b: 2 }
```

Can you differentiate what the difference is between the preceding two lines? What is a variable object and what is a constant object?

If an object is declared with const, it means only the object itself can't be used to point to another memory space:

```
const obj = {}
obj = {}        // compiler error
obj.key = ''   // valid
```

In the preceding code, we defined an `obj` constant. Later on, if we attempt to overwrite `obj`, the compiler will throw an error. However, if we modify its content via a key, it's still valid. Similarly, we can expect this behavior from an array:

```
const arr = []
arr = []       // compiler error
arr.push('A') // valid
```

You might find this behavior a bit strange, but it actually is designed pretty consistently for all objects and arrays when it comes to their initialization, comparison, and so on.

If you see an array or object defined with a `let` statement, it should tell you that they can be overwritten later on:

```
let obj = {}
let arr = []
```

This is the main difference between the `let` and `const` statements.

Modules

There's one thing a developer can't live without these days, which is code imported from another file. However, *JavaScript* didn't support this until *ES6* finally introduced a module system similar to what module loaders such as *AMD* or *CommonJS* provide. The idea is that we can export something from a file for reuse, as shown in this example:

```
const Title = () => <div>Hello World</div>
export default Title
```

The preceding code is quite common in a *React* application. Basically, it defines a `Title` component in a separate file and exports it as a default. From another file, we can import it and use it through an `import`, like so:

```
import Title from './Title'
const App = () => <Title />
```

This is the main mechanism for pulling all the files together and compiling them into a single `index.js` file because it actually imports all of them.

Sometimes, we also want to export other materials along with `default`:

```
const Title = () => <div>Hello World</div>
export default Title
const TitleType = "Component"
export { TitleType }
```

In the preceding code, we exported `Title` as `default`, and we also exported `TitleType` as a non-default. This means that we can cherry-pick things and import them individually:

```
import Title, { TitleType } from './Title'
```

This capability becomes handy when we store a bunch of related utility functionalities in a single file and export them one by one:

```
const fn1 = () => {}
const fn2 = () => {}
export { fn1, fn2 }
```

To avoid the name collision, upon import, we can use the aliasing import via the `as` keyword:

```
Import { fn1 as aliasFn1 } from './fns'
// we can use aliasFn1
```

Symbol

Symbol is a new *JavaScript* feature that sounds like a game term. In fact, it is a special primitive type. Normally, we could have a string as a property key:

```
obj['name'] = 3
```

Anyone who writes the preceding line can access the value stored under the name property. But what if we want to restrict access to only people who know a key? You may ask, "what do you mean by that? Isn't the "name" string public to anyone?" That is the point – we want to create a key that not everyone can recreate easily. Here's what we will do:

```
const Name = Symbol('name')
obj[Name] = 3
```

In the preceding code, a `Symbol` with the "name" string is created to serve as a key. We can still access this symbolized property under `obj` if we have the exact key. But it won't work if you create another key like that and try to access the property, like so:

```
const Name = Symbol('name')
obj[Name] = 4
```

Hmm, aren't we using the same code again? Why can't we access the same key? The answer lies in the following comparison:

```
Symbol('name') !== Symbol('name')
```

The preceding comparison between two `Symbol('name')` `statements` returns `false`! This means you can't expect to recreate the `"name"` key by writing it again; you can only have the original key you create in the first place or query through it from all registered keys in the system via `Symbol.for`:

```
Symbol.for('name') === Symbol.for('name')
```

Once we find the key in the system, we can then access the property:

```
const Name = Symbol.for('name')
obj[Name] = 4
```

Ahh. This is interesting, isn't it?

A symbol is a primitive that cannot be recreated and is guaranteed to be unique! This means that it can serve as a unique key to a door. If the key is not present, then the door can't be opened.

This becomes useful when we don't want any developer to mistakenly access some memory or assign a value. It also becomes useful to transfer this key to another project or repository in a unique way. I will show you an example of how *React* uses it in the next section.

So far, we have gone over a couple of topics from *ES6*, including arrow functions, object enhancement, template strings, destructuring, `let` and `const`, modules, and symbols. But there's actually more to *ES6*, such as promise, proxy, generators, and weak map. We used promise when we referred to an API and used proxy in *Chapter 9, Use Custom Hooks to Reuse Logic*.

One thing for sure is that *React* really takes advantage of the latest *JavaScript* language. If you practice them often, one thing you will find is that code becomes more expressive without losing its accuracy.

In the next section, we'll see how *React* uses materials from non-*JavaScript* languages, such as *CSS*.

Adopting CSS-in-JS approach

When we build an application in *React*, at one point, we need to find a way to apply *CSS* styles to our code, right? If you have *CSS* experience in the past, one approach we're familiar with is to use *CSS* classes to style styles. Consider the following *CSS* snippet stored in a file with a .css extension:

```css
h1 {
   color: red;
}
```

We can apply this style to a *React* element via a prop called className:

```jsx
const Title = () => {
   return <h1 className="title">Hello</h1>
}
```

> **Note**
>
> class is a reserved keyword for *JavaScript* and therefore can't be used.
> Instead, *React* chooses to use a different word, className.

Though this old method continues to work, there's one issue about the uniqueness of the title class. *CSS* can be applied to all the title elements on the screen, but it can't skip an element inside a component that we don't want to be styled. From the *CSS* perspective, the title class is exposed to be styled globally.

Using a component design, it's just natural that we would want to apply the style to this component only! For example, the title style we defined can be only valid inside the Title component. Believe it or not, having a scope is the foundation of the component design.

One way to make the style unique to the component is to bake the style inline along with the element using a style prop:

```jsx
const Title = () => {
   return <h1 style={{ color: "red" }}>Hello</h1>
}
```

But the problem of the preceding hardcoded approach is also quite obvious. It's just not feasible to write a large amount of styles inline. This is where the *CSS-in-JS* approach comes into play. The idea is to utilize a template string to write the *CSS* using the old method. Okay, we just introduced the template strings from one of the *ES6* features:

```
const css = '
  h1 { color: red; }
'
```

There's almost no learning curve to use the preceding string. Thus, this approach has been adopted by the community quickly and implemented by a couple of libraries, such as `styled-JSX` and `styled-components`. We will introduce both in this section, so let's get started.

styled-SX

`styled-JSX` is a *CSS-in-JS* library that allows us to write scoped *CSS* for a component where the style doesn't affect other components, thus allowing us to amend styles without worrying about making changes to other components on the screen.

Let's take the same `Title` component and see how it's done with `styled-JSX`:

```
const Title = () => (
  <>
    <h1>Hello</h1>
    <style jsx>{'
      h1 { color: red; }
    '}</style>
  </>
)
```

It introduces a special `style` tag with a `jsx` prop, and underneath it, the styles can be written as *CSS* code. The styles are only injected once, even if the `Title` component is used more than once.

This semi-inline approach of styles can be quite efficient when it comes to prototyping an application. Instead of putting the *CSS* inline with the component, we can put the styles in a separate file, like so:

```
import css from 'styled-jsx/css'
export default css'
  h1 {
    color: red;
  }
'
```

We can import it into the `Title` component:

```
import titleStyle from '../titleStyle'
const Title = () => (
  <>
    <h1>Hello</h1>
    <style jsx>{titleStyle}</style>
  </>
)
```

This gives us some freedom to write the CSS either inline or in a separate file.

One important thing to note is that the styles we wrote so far do not apply to child components by default:

```
const Child = () => <span>World</span>
const Title = () => (
  <>
    <h1>Hello <Child /></h1>
    <style jsx>{'
      span { color: green; }
    '}
  </>
}
```

The preceding code wouldn't make any span element displayed with a green color. To get it working, we can use a `global` attribute:

```
const Child = () => <span>World</span>
const Title = () => (
  <>
    <h1>Hello <Child /></h1>
    <style jsx global>{'
      h1 { color: red; }
      span { color: green; }
    '}
    </style>
  </>
)
```

styled-JSX is quite a unique library that makes styling easy in *React*. Moreover, since the styles are actually written in a *JavaScript* string, it can be manipulated at runtime. We'll demonstrate this feature in the next package, styled-components, since this feature works for both packages.

styled-components

There's another library implementing the *CSS-in-JS* strategy called `styled-components`. This book has adopted this approach for all examples requiring styles. Instead of using a `style` tag, it actually allows us to define the *CSS* in a separate component:

```
import styled from 'styled-components'
const TitleStyle = styled.h1'
  color: red;
'
const Title = () => {
  return (
    <TitleStyle>
      Hello World
    </TitleStyle>
  )
}
```

In the preceding code, `styled.h1` is a tagged template function that outputs a component with an embedded `h1` element.

Moreover, `styled-components` allows *CSS* to apply to the children by default, which is very different from the `styled-JSX` package:

```
const TitleStyle = styled.h1'
  color: red;
  span { color: green; }
'
const Child = () => <span>World</span>
const Title = () => {
  return (
    <TitleStyle>
      Hello <Child />
    </TitleStyle>
  )
}
```

The preceding code sets the `span` element with a green color. This reminds us of Sass or SCSS code.

One interesting benefit that the *CSS-in-JS* solution provides is that the *JavaScript* string can be blended with other *JavaScript* expressions to support dynamic styles at runtime:

```
const fontSize = (props) =>
  props.big ? '3em' : '1.5em'
const TitleStyle = styled.h1'
  font-size: ${fontSize};
'
const Title = ({ big }) => {
  return (
    <TitleStyle big={big}>
      Hello World!
    </TitleStyle>
  )
}
```

The preceding code defines a `big` prop that can be sent to the `TitleStyle` component where, based on the `big` value, `fontSize` can be switched between `3em` and `1.5em`.

The dynamic *CSS* support makes it possible to create themeable components quite easily in *React*, and also opens the door for animating components that require a value change over time.

Now that we have seen how *React* brings *CSS* into *JavaScript* to blend the two technologies together, let's move on to *HTML* and see how it can be brought into *React*.

Going from HTML to JSX

One barrier for a developer adopting *React*, especially if they are used to working with other web technologies, is that *HTML* isn't imported into the project anymore. There's not a file with a `.html` extension, except the entry `index.html` file, which most of the time only has one line of *HTML* inside, like so:

```
<div id="root">loading...</div>
```

But that's it. If there was a project manager that liked to review *HTML* or even work on it, they can't do that anymore. This missing *HTML* file could be one of the reasons why teams are hesitant to adopt *React*.

However, *HTML* has a similar problem to *CSS*. They don't have scopes that we have in programming languages. Even worse, a piece of *HTML*, once written, is almost turned into *DOM* elements instantly. So, a component-based system has to come up with a way to add a layer in between.

How did *React* solve this problem? It chose to take the *HTML* in – no surprise. But one amazing job that *React* did is that it kept the experience of writing these statements as close as possible to *HTML*. Technically, *React* made the smooth transformation from a piece of *HTML* to a piece of *JavaScript* code possible. Sometimes, we don't notice this, nor can we tell the difference:

```
return <h1 title="Title">Hello World</h1>
```

The preceding code is what we use inside a function component. The format does look like a piece of *HTML*. What's seen by the compiler is the following:

```
return React.createElement(
   'h1', { title: "Title" }, "Hello World"
)
```

After the compiler transformation, it becomes a *JavaScript* expression of a `createElement` function, taking three input arguments.

The magic of how this transformation happens is done through a compiler with a *Babel* plugin. When the compiler builds the code, Babel converts the code into an abstract syntax tree, a token format, and then stitches them back together and puts them into the *JavaScript* format.

> **Note**
>
> If you are interested in knowing what a compiler does, you can visit `https://babeljs.io/repl` and try it out yourself.

We are going to take a look at this `createElement` function closely now. The first input argument of the `createElement` function is the `type` of the element, which is taken from the element tag `h1`. The second one is the `props`, which is an object containing the `title` property. Last, but not least, the third one is the `children`; in our case, it's a string containing `"Hello World"`. Let's walk through these input arguments in more detail, since each of them is an essential part of *React*!

Props

The `props` input argument is one of the most important *React* mechanisms. We have been talking about props all the time, and this is where they receive their first-hand values. It's because `createElement` is a *JavaScript* function that we can wire any *JavaScript* expression to the props:

```
const Title = ({ title }) => {
   const [count] = useState(0)
```

```
  return React.createElement(
    'h1', { title, count }, "Hello World"
  )
}
```

In the preceding code, it's apparent now how a `title` prop and a `count` state are sent to `createElement` as part of the props.

This also explains why we can't use the `class` reserved word as the prop to style the component:

```
// code below wouldn't work
const Title = () => {
  return React.createElement(
    'h1', { class: "title" }, "Hello World"
  )
}
```

The preceding code would raise a compiler error due to the `class` key.

Children

The `children` input argument is the reason that we can nest one element under another element:

```
  return (
    <h1>
      <span>
        Hello World
      </span>
    </h1>
  )
```

What the compiler sees is the following:

```
  return React.createElement(
    'h1', null, React.createElement(
      'span', null, "Hello World"
    )
  )
```

Note from the preceding output that there are two usages of `createElement`, one for the `h1` element and one for the child `span` element. The second `createElement` function is used as the `children` argument of the first `createElement` function.

Now, it's not too difficult to see a long list of elements nested and returned from a component via `createElement` functions. Technically, even without the compiler's help, you can code your component manually with this nested writing.

Though a single element can be nested under, there can be cases where more than one element needs to be nested under another one:

```
return (
  <ul>
    {['Apple', 'Orange'].map(v => <li>{v}</li>)}
  </ul>
)
```

For the preceding *JavaScript* expression involving an array, the array would be sent to the `children` of `createElement`:

```
return React.createElement(
  'ul',
  null,
  ['apple', 'orange'].map((v) =>
    React.createElement('li', null, v)
  )
)
```

Essentially, the `children` input argument can support the following formats:

- A `"Hello World"` string
- A single element via `createElement`
- An array of elements with either of the preceding format

React also allows you to add any number of children in another way:

```
return React.createElement(
  'ul',
  null,
  React.createElement('li', null, 'apple'),
  React.createElement('li', null, 'orange')
)
```

In the preceding code, we can stack the children in the input argument list, starting from the third input argument.

Element type

An element type, the first input argument to createElement, can be a simple string representing an *HTML* tag, such as h1 and span. However, it can also take other formats, such as a function:

```
const Child = () => <h1>Hello World</h1>
const Title = () => {
  return <Child />
}
```

What the compiler sees of the preceding code is the following:

```
const Child = () =>
  React.createElement("h1", null, "Hello World")
const Title = () => React.createElement(Child, null)
```

Note Child in the preceding code – the function itself is sent to createElement as the element type! This is how *React* allows you to create an element out of a custom component. Because of this, it means we can support a dynamic element type at runtime:

```
const Child1 = () => <h1>Hello</h1>
const Child2 = () => <h1>World</h1>
const Title = ({ flag }) => {
  const Child = flag ? Child1 : Child2
  return <Child />
}
```

In the preceding code, instead of returning either <Child1 /> or <Child2 />, we first determine the type of Child component at the runtime and then return the instance from this <Child /> component. This is all possible because the component type is a *JavaScript* variable:

```
const Child1 = () => React.createElement(
  "h1", null, "Hello"
)
const Child2 = () => React.createElement(
  "h1", null, "World"
)
const Title = ({ flag }) => {
  const Child = flag ? Child1 : Child2
  return React.createElement(Child, null)
}
```

The preceding code confirms what the compiler sees. The Child component type is determined at runtime.

Now that we have seen the `createElement` function and its three input arguments, let's take a close look at what it returns.

React element

As the `createElement` name indicates, the function returns a root element with a tree of elements under it.

Is the element a *DOM* element? No, it's called a *React* element. Though the *React* documentation doesn't talk too much about it, we'll reveal it a bit briefly here:

```
{
  $$typeof: Symbol.for('react.element'),
  type: type,
  props: props,
}
```

The preceding code is a short definition of the *React* element definition. As you can see, it's basically an object. We've been introduced to `type` and `props`, but what the heck is `$$typeof`? Apparently, this is not something that *React* wants anyone to tamper with.

It turns out *React* supports various categories of elements. For the lack of a better word, let's call `$$typeof` another type, an internal type. The one we used most often was `react.element`, and it's defined as a `Symbol`. We just introduced `Symbol` in the previous section. Basically, `react.element` is a unique primitive value that, once created, can be used but not changed.

You may ask, "what are other types are there?" Actually, there are two dozen of them; here are just a few that might interest you:

- `react.element`
- `react.portal`
- `react.fragment`
- `react.provider`
- `react.suspense`
- `react.memo`
- `react.lazy`

Why do we need all these different types?

Most of the application implementation is more or less around updating a `react.element`, but when it comes to special cases, it requires a different updating algorithm. Let's take a look at the following example:

```
import { memo } from 'react'
const App = memo(() => {
  return (
    <Provider value={3}>
      <>
        <div>One</div>
        <div>Second</div>
      </>
    </Provider>
  )
})
```

In the preceding code, `Provider` creates an element with a `react.provider` type. Under it, `<>` creates an element with a `react.fragment` type, and under it, `div` creates two elements with a `react.element` type. The entire component is wrapped in a `memo` element with a `react.memo` type. This gives you a rough idea of where different *React* elements are used.

In short, what returns from the JSX code block are *React* elements. These *React* elements are what is fed into the *React* engine.

Summary

In this chapter, we started with the function of *React* in web development. We went into three aspects of it. First, we went through the latest *ES6* features of *JavaScript*, such as the arrow function and template strings. Next, we learned the *CSS-in-JS* approach to bring *CSS* into *JavaScript*, using libraries such as `styled-JSX` and `styled-components`. Last, but not least, we learned how *HTML*-like JSX code is transformed and returned as *React* elements. All in all, we saw how *React* pulls all these resources together, including *JavaScript*, *CSS*, and *HTML*, to help us build a site.

Questions and answers

The following are some questions and answers to refresh your knowledge:

1. What is *React*?

   It's a tool that allows us to design a component and manage its update with a render engine.

2. What is *JavaScript ES6*?

   JavaScript has all the latest features published as *ES6*. *React* takes advantage of them, using features such as the arrow function, template strings, and destructuring. Using them in your project would make your code more efficient, expressive, and maintainable.

3. What's *CSS-in-JS*?

   CSS-in-JS refers to one opinionated but popular way to apply styles to a *React* component. The styles applied are localized to the component and don't collide with any other components. Moreover, the styles can be wired with any *JavaScript* expression to support dynamic styles at runtime.

4. What is JSX code?

   React allows us to use JSX code to write *HTML*-like code. Practically, they look quite similar, except JSX allows us to transform these statements into native *JavaScript* expressions that accept element types, props, and children from the input argument and return *React* elements that the engine can put into effect.

Index

W

Packt.com

Subscribe to our online digital library for full access to over 7,000 books and videos, as well as industry leading tools to help you plan your personal development and advance your career. For more information, please visit our website.

Why subscribe?

- Spend less time learning and more time coding with practical eBooks and Videos from over 4,000 industry professionals

- Improve your learning with Skill Plans built especially for you

- Get a free eBook or video every month

- Fully searchable for easy access to vital information

- Copy and paste, print, and bookmark content

Did you know that Packt offers eBook versions of every book published, with PDF and ePub files available? You can upgrade to the eBook version at packt.com and as a print book customer, you are entitled to a discount on the eBook copy. Get in touch with us at customercare@packtpub.com for more details.

At www.packt.com, you can also read a collection of free technical articles, sign up for a range of free newsletters, and receive exclusive discounts and offers on Packt books and eBooks.

Other Books You May Enjoy

If you enjoyed this book, you may be interested in these other books by Packt:

Simplify Testing with React Testing Library

Scottie Crump

ISBN: 978-1-80056-445-9

- Explore React Testing Library and its use cases
- Get to grips with the RTL ecosystem
- Apply jest-dom to enhance your tests using RTL
- Gain the confidence you need to create tests that don't break with changes using RTL
- Integrate Cucumber and Cypress into your test suite
- Use TDD to drive the process of writing tests
- Apply your existing React knowledge for using RTL

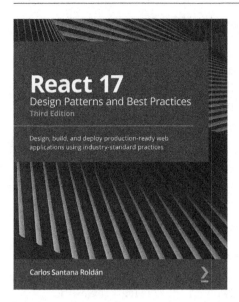

React 17 Design Patterns and Best Practices

Carlos Santana Roldán

ISBN: 978-1-80056-044-4

- Get to grips with the techniques of styling and optimizing React components
- Create components using the new React Hooks
- Get to grips with the new React Suspense technique and using GraphQL in your projects
- Use server-side rendering to make applications load faster
- Write a comprehensive set of tests to create robust and maintainable code
- Build high-performing applications by optimizing components

Packt is searching for authors like you

If you're interested in becoming an author for Packt, please visit `authors.`
`packtpub.com` and apply today. We have worked with thousands of developers and
tech professionals, just like you, to help them share their insight with the global tech
community. You can make a general application, apply for a specific hot topic that we are
recruiting an author for, or submit your own idea.

Hi!

I am Fang Jin, author of *Designing React Hooks the Right Way*. I really hope you enjoyed
reading this book and found it useful for increasing your productivity and efficiency in
React.

It would really help me (and other potential readers!) if you could leave a review on
Amazon sharing your thoughts on *Designing React Hooks the Right Way*.

Go to the link below or scan the QR code to leave your review: `https://packt.`
`link/r/1803235950/`

Your review will help me to understand what's worked well in this book, and what could be improved upon for future editions, so it really is appreciated.

Best Wishes,

Fang Jin

Made in the USA
Coppell, TX
29 June 2022

79384141R10155